Presented to:

P Marlene

Date:

21
DAYS
BUILDING
HEALTHY
HABITS
FOR *Women*

The quoted ideas expressed in this book (but not Scripture verses) are not, in all cases, exact quotations, as some have been edited for clarity and brevity. In all cases, the author has attempted to maintain the speaker's original intent. In some cases, quoted material for this book was obtained from secondary sources, primarily print media. While every effort was made to ensure the accuracy of these sources, the accuracy cannot be guaranteed. For additions, deletions, corrections, or clarifications in future editions of this text, please write Freeman-Smith, LLC.

Scripture quotations are taken from:

The Holy Bible, King James Version (KJV)

The Holy Bible, New King James Version (NKJV) Copyright © 1982 by Thomas Nelson, Inc. Used by permission.

The Holman Christian Standard Bible™ (HOLMAN CSB) Copyright © 1999, 2000, 2001 by Holman Bible Publishers. Used by permission.

Cover Design by Kim Russell / Wahoo Designs
Page Layout by Bart Dawson

ISBN 1-58334-327-X

Printed in the United States of America

21
DAYS
BUILDING
HEALTHY
HABITS
FOR *Women*

Table of Contents

Introduction

Maybe you've heard the old saying that it takes 21 days to change a habit. It's a common-sense idea that makes a valid point: If you can do anything for 21 straight days, then there's a very good chance you can keep doing it on the 22nd day, and the 23rd, and the 24th, and beyond.

If you thought that you could establish a number of healthy habits, would you be willing to carve out a few minutes each day for the next three weeks in order to find out? If you answered yes, congratulations! You are about to embark on a grand adventure.

This book contains 21 chapters, each of which contains a devotional message that addresses a healthy habit for thoughtful Christian women like you. If you read each devotional carefully—and if you implement the ideas that you find there—you can have a profound impact on your own life and upon the lives of your loved ones.

If you're like most women, you've already tried, perhaps on many occasions, to form healthier habits. You've employed your own willpower in a noble effort to create a new, improved, healthier you. You've probably tried to improve various aspects of your spiritual, physical, or emotional health. Perhaps you've gone on diets or made New Year's resolutions or tried the latest self-help fad in an attempt to finally make important changes in your life. And if you're like most women, you've been successful . . . for a while. But eventually, those old familiar habits came creeping back into your life, and the improvements that you had made proved to be temporary. This book is intended to help you build a series of healthy habits for your Christian walk . . . and make those habits stick.

During the next 21 days, you will be asked to depend less upon your own willpower and more upon God's power. For three short weeks, you'll be asked to focus on three major areas of your life: spiritual health, physical health, and emotional health. When you form a working relationship with God, you'll be amazed by the things that the two of you, working together, can do in 21 short days.

PART 1

Your
SPIRITUAL
HEALTH

Nothing is more important than the condition of your spiritual health.

DAY 1

FORMING THE HABIT OF . . .

Bible Study

*All Scripture is inspired by God and is profitable
for teaching, for rebuking, for correcting,
for training in righteousness, so that the man
of God may be complete, equipped for
every good work.*

2 Timothy 3:16-17 Holman CSB

Have you established the habit of reading your Bible every single day of the week with no exceptions? The answer to this simple question will determine, to a surprising extent, the quality of your life and the direction of your faith.

As you begin to establish healthy habits during the next 21 days, you must decide whether God's Word will be a bright spotlight that guides your path every day or a tiny nightlight that occasionally flickers in the dark. The decision to study the Bible—or not—is yours and yours alone, but make no mistake: how you choose to use the Bible will have a profound impact on you and your loved ones.

> Since the Christian's Point of Reference is the Bible, it's a happy couple who look there for guidance.
>
> Ruth Bell Graham

George Mueller observed, "The vigor of our spiritual lives will be in exact proportion to the place held by the Bible in our lives and in our thoughts." Think of it like this: the more you use your Bible, the more God uses you.

God's Word is unlike any other book, and you should treat it that way. As a Christian, you are instructed to study the Bible and meditate upon its meaning for your life. But far too many Bibles are laid aside by well-intentioned believers who would like to study the Bible if they could "just find the time." If you can't seem to "find" the time to engage in a serious study of God's Word, it's time to reorganize your priorities.

Perhaps your bookshelf is filled with Bibles that are read infrequently. If so, remember the old saying, "A Bible in the hand is worth two in the bookcase." Or perhaps you're one of those people who are simply "too busy" to find time for a daily dose of prayer and Bible study. If so, remember the old adage, "It's hard to stumble when you're on your knees."

God's Word can be a roadmap to a place of righteousness and abundance. Make it your roadmap. God's wisdom can be a light to guide your steps. Claim it as your light today, tomorrow, and every day of your life—and then walk confidently in the footsteps of God's only begotten Son.

Study the Bible and observe how the persons behaved and how God dealt with them. There is explicit teaching on every condition of life.

Corrie ten Boom

Nobody ever outgrows Scripture; the book widens and deepens with our years.

C. H. Spurgeon

The balance of affirmation and discipline, freedom and restraint, encouragement and warning is different for each child and season and generation, yet the absolutes of God's Word are necessary and trustworthy no matter how mercuric the time.

Gloria Gaither

Heaven and earth will pass away, but My words will never pass away.

Matthew 24:35 Holman CSB

Man shall not live by bread alone, but by every word that proceeds from the mouth of God.

Matthew 4:4 NKJV

For the word of God is living and effective and sharper than any two-edged sword, penetrating as far as to divide soul, spirit, joints, and marrow; it is a judge of the ideas and thoughts of the heart.

Hebrews 4:12 Holman CSB

For I am not ashamed of the gospel, because it is God's power for salvation to everyone who believes.

Romans 1:16 Holman CSB

MY VALUES

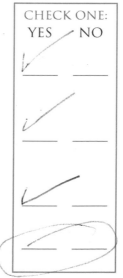

CHECK ONE:
YES / NO

I believe that it is important to read
the Bible every day.

I believe the Bible is God's instruction book to
all of mankind and for my family.

I consider regular Bible study to be an important
source of wisdom.

I have a systematic plan for studying the Bible.

My Prayer

*Dear Lord, I praise You for Your Holy Word.
Let the Bible be my guide for life here on earth
and for life eternal. And, let me be a worthy example
to others, Lord, so that they might see my love for
You reflected in everything that I say and do.
Amen*

What I Can Do

_____

_____

_____

_____

_____

_____

_____

_____

_____

_____

_____

_____

_____

_____

_____

_____

_____

_____

_____

_____

SIGN ON!

_____

IF YOU AGREE TO THE ABOVE PLANS, PLEASE SIGN YOUR NAME.

FORMING THE HABIT OF . . .

Prayer

And everything—whatever you ask in prayer, believing—you will receive.

Matthew 21:22 HOLMAN CSB

I s the habit of prayer an integral part of your daily life or is it a hit-or-miss routine? Do you "pray without ceasing," or is your prayer life an afterthought? Do you regularly pray in the solitude of the early morning darkness, or do you bow your head only when others are watching?

Your search to discover the abundance and peace that God has in store for you is not a destination; it is a journey that unfolds day by day. And, that's exactly how often you should seek direction from your Creator: one day at a time, each day followed by the next, without exception.

Daily prayer and meditation is a matter of will and habit. You must willingly organize your time by carving out quiet moments with God, and you must form the habit of daily worship. When you do, you'll discover that no time is more precious than the silent moments you spend with your Heavenly Father.

> When you ask God to do something, don't ask timidly; put your whole heart into it.
>
> Marie T. Freeman

God promises that the prayers of righteous men and women can accomplish great things. God promises that He answers prayer (although His answers are not always in accordance with our desires). God invites us to be still and to feel His presence. So pray. Start praying before the sun comes up and keep praying until you fall off to sleep at night. Pray about matters great and small; and be watchful for the answers that God most assuredly sends your way.

The quality of your spiritual life will be in direct proportion to the quality of your prayer life. Prayer changes things, and it changes you. Today, instead of turning things over in your mind, turn them over to God in prayer. Instead of worrying about your next decision, ask God to lead the way. Don't limit your prayers to meals or to bedtime; pray constantly. God is listening; He wants to hear from you; and you most certainly need to hear from Him.

The center of power is not to be found in summit meetings or in peace conferences. It is not in Peking or Washington or the United Nations, but rather where a child of God prays in the power of the Spirit for God's will to be done in her life, in her home, and in the world around her.

Ruth Bell Graham

When there is a matter that requires definite prayer, pray until you believe God and until you can thank Him for His answer.

Hannah Whitall Smith

I live in the spirit of prayer; I pray as I walk, when I lie down, and when I rise. And, the answers are always coming.

George Mueller

As we join together in prayer, we draw on God's enabling might in a way that multiplies our own efforts many times over.

Shirley Dobson

And everything—whatever you ask in prayer, believing—you will receive.

Matthew 21:22 Holman CSB

Rejoice always! Pray constantly. Give thanks in everything, for this is God's will for you in Christ Jesus.

1 Thessalonians 5:16-18 Holman CSB

Therefore I want the men in every place to pray, lifting up holy hands without anger or argument.

1 Timothy 2:8 Holman CSB

The intense prayer of the righteous is very powerful.

James 5:16 Holman CSB

For More Thoughts About Prayer, Please Turn to Page 146

MY VALUES

	CHECK ONE:	
	YES	NO

I understand that prayer strengthens my
relationship with God.

_____ _____

I trust that God will care for me, even when it
seems that my prayers have gone unanswered.

_____ _____

I believe that my prayers have the power
to change my circumstances, my perspective,
and my future.

_____ _____

My Prayer

*Dear Lord, I will be a woman of prayer.
I will pray about matters great and small. I
will bring my concerns to You, Father. I will listen
for Your voice, and I will follow in
the footsteps of Your Son.
Amen*

What I Can Do

_____

_____

_____

_____

_____

_____

_____

_____

_____

_____

_____

_____

_____

_____

_____

_____

_____

_____

SIGN ON!

_____

IF YOU AGREE TO THE ABOVE PLANS, PLEASE SIGN YOUR NAME.

DAY 3

FORMING THE HABIT OF . . .

Obedience

I have sought You with all my heart;
don't let me wander from Your commands.

Psalm 119:10 Holman CSB

God's laws are eternal and unchanging. Obedience to those laws inevitably leads to abundance, peace and joy while disobedience inevitably leads to disaster. God has given us a guidebook for abundant life; that book is the Holy Bible. It contains thorough instructions which, if followed, lead to fulfillment, righteousness, and salvation. But, if we choose to ignore God's commandments, the results are as predictable as they are tragic.

How can we demonstrate our love for God? By placing Christ squarely at the center of our lives. Jesus said that if we are to love Him, we must obey His commandments (John 14: 15). Thus, our obedience to the Master is an expression of our love for Him.

> Obey God one step at a time, then the next step will come into view.
>
> Catherine Marshall

In Ephesians 2:10 we read, "For we are His workmanship, created in Christ Jesus for good works" (NKJV). These words are instructive: We are not saved by good works, but for good works. Good works are not the root, but rather the fruit of our salvation.

When we seek righteousness in our own lives—and when we seek the companionship of those who do likewise—we reap the spiritual rewards that God intends for our lives. When we form the habit of obedience—and when we choose to follow in the footsteps of God's only begotten Son—we honor our Creator. When we live righteously and according to God's commandments, He blesses us in ways that we cannot fully understand.

Today, take every step of your journey with God as your traveling companion. Read His Word and obey His commandments. Support only those activities that further God's kingdom and your spiritual growth. Be an example of righteous living to your friends, to your neighbors, and to your loved ones. Then, reap the blessings that God has promised to all those who live according to His will and His Word.

A life of obedience is not a life of following a list of do's and don'ts, but it is allowing God to be original in our lives.

Vonette Bright

The Christian is never to be out of the control of the Holy Spirit.

Kay Arthur

God will see to it that we understand as much truth as we are willing to obey.

Elisabeth Elliot

Perfect obedience would be perfect happiness, if only we had perfect confidence in the power we were obeying.

Corrie ten Boom

Now by this we know that we know Him, if we keep His commandments.

1 John 2:3 NKJV

And the world with its lust is passing away, but the one who does God's will remains forever.

1 John 2:17 Holman CSB

But whoever keeps His word, truly the love of God is perfected in him. By this we know that we are in Him. He who says he abides in Him ought himself also to walk just as He walked.

1 John 2:5-6 NKJV

Therefore, get your minds ready for action, being self-disciplined, and set your hope completely on the grace to be brought to you at the revelation of Jesus Christ. As obedient children, do not be conformed to the desires of your former ignorance but, as the One who called you is holy, you also are to be holy in all your conduct.

1 Peter 1:13-15 Holman CSB

For More Thoughts About Obedience, Please Turn to Page 144

MY VALUES

	CHECK ONE:	
	YES	NO

I will study God's Word.

I will strive to obey God's commandments.

I will associate with fellow believers who,
by their words and actions, encourage me
to obey God.

I will not willingly put myself in situations where
I might be easily tempted to disobey God.

My Prayer

*Dear Lord, make me a woman who is obedient to Your
Word. Let me live according to Your commandments.
Direct my path far from the temptations and
distractions of this world. And, let me discover
Your will and follow it, Lord, this day and always.
Amen*

What I Can Do

_____

_____

_____

_____

_____

_____

_____

_____

_____

_____

_____

_____

_____

_____

_____

_____

_____

_____

SIGN ON!

_____

IF YOU AGREE TO THE ABOVE PLANS, PLEASE SIGN YOUR NAME.

FORMING THE HABIT OF . . .

Matthew 6:14-15 [handwritten]

Forgiveness

Matthew 5:44-45 [handwritten]

All bitterness, anger and wrath, insult and slander must be removed from you, along with all wickedness. And be kind and compassionate to one another, forgiving one another, just as God also forgave you in Christ.

Ephesians 4:31-32 Holman CSB

Have you formed the habit of forgiving everybody (including yourself) as soon as possible? Hopefully so. Christ understood the importance of forgiveness when He commanded, "Love your enemies and pray for those who persecute you" (Matthew 5:43-44 NIV). But sometimes, forgiveness is difficult indeed.

When we have been injured or embarrassed, we feel the urge to strike back and to hurt the ones who have hurt us. But Christ instructs us to do otherwise. Christ teaches us that forgiveness is God's way and that mercy is an integral part of God's plan for our lives. In short, we are commanded to weave the thread of forgiveness into the very fabric of our lives.

Do you invest more time than you should reliving the past? Are you troubled by feelings of anger, bitterness, envy, or regret? Do you harbor ill will against someone whom you simply can't seem to forgive? If so, it's time to finally get serious about forgiveness.

> Forgiveness is contagious. First you forgive them, and pretty soon, they'll forgive you, too.
>
> Marie T. Freeman

When someone hurts you, the act of forgiveness is difficult, but necessary. Until you forgive, you are trapped in a prison of your own creation. But what if you have tried to forgive and simply can't seem to do so? The solution to your dilemma is this: you simply must make forgiveness a higher priority in your life.

Most of us don't spend too much time thinking about forgiveness; we worry, instead, about the injustices we have suffered and the people who inflicted them. God has a better plan: He wants us to live in the present, not the past, and He knows that in order to do so, we must forgive those who have harmed us.

Have you made forgiveness a high priority? Have you sincerely asked God to forgive you for your inability to forgive others? Have you genuinely prayed that those feelings of hatred and anger might be swept from your heart? If so, congratulations. If not, perhaps it's time to rearrange your priorities . . . and perhaps it's time to free yourself from the chains of bitterness and regret.

Forgiveness is actually the best revenge because it not only sets us free from the person we forgive, but it frees us to move into all that God has in store for us.

Stormie Omartian

Only God in Christ has the power to forgive sin. But you and I must confess it to Him personally, specifically, and honestly if we want to receive forgiveness.

Anne Graham Lotz

Grudges are like hand grenades; it is wise to release them before they destroy you.

Barbara Johnson

And forgive us our sins, for we ourselves also forgive everyone in debt to us.

Luke 11:4 Holman CSB

A person's insight gives him patience, and his virtue is to overlook an offense.

Proverbs 19:11 Holman CSB

Be merciful, just as your Father also is merciful.

Luke 6:36 Holman CSB

See to it that no one repays evil for evil to anyone, but always pursue what is good for one another and for all.

1 Thessalonians 5:15 Holman CSB

For More Thoughts About Forgiveness, Please Turn to Page 148

MY VALUES

	CHECK ONE:	
	YES	NO

I acknowledge the important role that forgiveness plays in my life.

_____ _____

I will strive to forgive those who have hurt me, even when doing so is difficult.

_____ _____

I understand that forgiveness is a marathon (not a sprint), and I will prayerfully ask God to help me move beyond the emotions of bitterness and regret.

_____ _____

I will ask God to forgive my own shortcomings, and I will forgive myself for the mistakes that I have made.

_____ _____

My Prayer

*Dear Lord, let forgiveness rule my heart,
even when forgiveness is difficult. Let me be
Your obedient servant, Lord, and let me be a woman
who forgives others just as You have forgiven me.
Amen*

What I Can Do

_____

SIGN ON!

_____

IF YOU AGREE TO THE ABOVE PLANS, PLEASE SIGN YOUR NAME.

FORMING THE HABIT OF . . .

Stewardship

Based on the gift they have received,
everyone should use it to serve others,
as good managers of the varied grace of God.
1 Peter 4:10 Holman CSB

As believers, we are challenged to form the habit of stewardship. We are commanded (not advised, not encouraged, commanded!) to be faithful stewards of the gifts and talents that God has given us. But we live in a world that encourages us to do otherwise. Ours is a society that is filled to the brim with countless opportunities to squander our time and our talents. But we must beware: God instructs us never to squander the gifts that He bestows upon us.

Christian stewardship may be defined as "the proper management of one's resources for the glory of God." And for thoughtful believers, stewardship isn't a hit-or-miss proposition, it's a way of thinking and a way of living. Oswald Chambers advised, "Never support an experience which does not have God as its source, and faith in God as its result." And so it is with our service. When we return to God that which is rightfully His, we experience the spiritual growth that always accompanies obedience to Him. But, when we attempt to shortchange our Creator, either materially or spiritually, we distance ourselves from God. The consequences of our disobedience are sadly predictable.

> God will withdraw resources from the poor stewards, as related in Matthew 25, and give it to the good stewards.
>
> Bill Bright

All of us have special gifts, and you are no exception. Today, accept this challenge: value the talent that God has given you, nourish it, make it grow, and share it with the world. After all, the best way to say "Thank You" for God's gifts is to use them.

How will you honor God today? Will you honor Him with the best you have to offer? Will you tithe the firstfruits of your harvest? Will you praise God not only with your words but also with your deeds? If you do, you will be blessed by a loving and righteous Father.

Each day provides a fresh opportunity to honor God with your prayers, with your praise, with your testimony, and with your service. Does the level of your stewardship honor the One who has given you everything? If so, rest assured: God will bless you because of your obedience. And if your stewardship has been somehow deficient, the best day to change is this one.

The Lord has abundantly blessed me all of my life. I'm not trying to pay Him back for all of His wonderful gifts; I just realize that He gave them to me to give away.

Lisa Whelchel

Not everyone possesses boundless energy or a conspicuous talent. We are not equally blessed with great intellect or physical beauty or emotional strength. But we have all been given the same ability to be faithful.

Gigi Graham Tchividjian

God has given you special talents—now it's your turn to give them back to God.

Marie T. Freeman

Anyone finding his life will lose it, and anyone losing his life because of Me will find it.

Matthew 10:39 Holman CSB

Well done, good and faithful servant; you were faithful over a few things, I will make you ruler over many things. Enter into the joy of your lord.

Matthew 25:21 NKJV

There is therefore now no condemnation to those who are in Christ Jesus, who do not walk according to the flesh, but according to the Spirit.

Romans 8:1 NKJV

Let a man so consider us, as servants of Christ and stewards of the mysteries of God. Moreover it is required in stewards that one be found faithful.

1 Corinthians 4:1-2 NKJV

MY VALUES

	CHECK ONE:	
	YES	NO

I understand the importance of being a good
steward of my time, my talent, and my resources.

I trust that all my resources come from God,
and I know that He deserves the firstfruits
of my labors.

I trust that when I am a good steward of my
resources, God will bless my endeavors
and my family.

My Prayer

*Dear Lord, make me a faithful steward of my
possessions. I trust, Father, that You will provide for
me now and throughout eternity. And I will obey Your
commandment that I give sacrificially to the needs of
Your Church. Thank You, Lord, for Your gifts.
Use my tithe as a blessing to others so that Your will
might be done today and forever.*
Amen

What I Can Do

_____

_____

_____

_____

_____

_____

_____

_____

_____

_____

_____

_____

_____

_____

_____

_____

_____

_____

_____

_____

_____

SIGN ON!

_____

IF YOU AGREE TO THE ABOVE PLANS, PLEASE SIGN YOUR NAME.

FORMING THE HABIT OF . . .

Worship

But an hour is coming, and is now here,
when the true worshipers will worship the
Father in spirit and truth. Yes, the Father wants
such people to worship Him. God is Spirit,
and those who worship Him must worship
in spirit and truth.

John 4:23-24 Holman CSB

How often do you attend church: regularly or sporadically? And just as importantly, why do you attend church? Is it because of your sincere desire to worship and to praise God? Hopefully so. Yet far too many Christians attend worship services because they believe they are "supposed to go to church" or because they feel "pressured" to attend. Still others go to church for "social" reasons. But make no mistake: the best reason to attend church is out of a sincere desire to please God, to praise God, to experience God, and to discern God's will for your lives.

Some people may tell you that they don't engage in worship. Don't believe them. All of mankind is engaged in worship. The question is not whether we worship, but what we worship. Wise people choose to worship God. When they do, they are blessed with a plentiful harvest of joy, peace, and abundance. Other people choose to distance themselves from God by foolishly worshiping things that are intended to bring personal gratification but not spiritual gratification. Such choices often have tragic consequences.

> Worship and worry cannot live in the same heart; they are mutually exclusive.
>
> Ruth Bell Graham

If we place our love for material possessions or social status above our love for God—or if we yield to the countless temptations of this world—we find ourselves engaged in a struggle between good and evil, a clash between God and Satan. Our responses to these struggles have implications that echo throughout our families and throughout our communities.

How can we ensure that we cast our lot with God? We do so, in part, by the practice of regular, purposeful worship in the company of fellow believers. When we worship God faithfully and fervently, we are blessed. When we fail to worship God, for whatever reason, we forfeit the spiritual gifts that might otherwise be ours.

We must worship our heavenly Father, not just with our words, but also with deeds. We must honor Him, praise Him, and obey Him. As we seek to find purpose and meaning for our lives, we must first seek His purpose and His will. For believers, God comes first. Always first.

It's our privilege to not only raise our hands in worship but also to combine the visible with the invisible in a rising stream of praise and adoration sent directly to our Father.

Shirley Dobson

In Biblical worship you do not find the repetition of a phrase; instead, you find the worshipers rehearsing the character of God and His ways, reminding Him of His faithfulness and His wonderful promises.

Kay Arthur

Spiritual worship is focusing all we are on all He is.

Beth Moore

If anyone is thirsty, he should come to Me and drink!

John 7:37 Holman CSB

Worship the Lord your God and . . . serve Him only.

Matthew 4:10 Holman CSB

And every day they devoted themselves to meeting together in the temple complex, and broke bread from house to house. They ate their food with gladness and simplicity of heart, praising God and having favor with all the people. And every day the Lord added those being saved to them.

Acts 2:46-47 Holman CSB

So that at the name of Jesus every knee should bow—of those who are in heaven and on earth and under the earth—and every tongue should confess that Jesus Christ is Lord, to the glory of God the Father.

Philippians 2:10-11 Holman CSB

For More Thoughts About Worship, Please Turn to Page 156

MY VALUES

	CHECK ONE:	
	YES	NO

I will consider each day an opportunity to praise God and to worship Him.

_____ _____

I will be actively involved in my church.

_____ _____

I will consider praise and worship to be a regular part of my day.

_____ _____

I will worship God in spirit and truth.

_____ _____

My Prayer

*When I worship You, Dear Lord, You set my path—
and my heart—straight. Let this day and every day be
a time of worship. Whether I am in Your house
or simply going about my daily activities, let me
worship You, not only with words and deeds, but also
with my heart. In the quiet moments of the day,
I will praise You for creating me, loving me,
guiding me, and saving me.*
Amen

What I Can Do

SIGN ON!

IF YOU AGREE TO THE ABOVE PLANS, PLEASE SIGN YOUR NAME.

FORMING THE HABIT OF . . .

Praise
and
Thanksgiving

It is good to give thanks to the Lord,
And to sing praises to Your name,
O Most High.

Psalm 92:1 NKJV

As believing Christians, we are blessed beyond measure. God sent His only Son to die for our sins. And, God has given us the priceless gifts of eternal love and eternal life. We, in turn, are instructed to approach our Heavenly Father with reverence and thanksgiving. But sometimes, in the crush of everyday living, we simply don't stop long enough to pause and thank our Creator for the countless blessings He has bestowed upon us.

When we slow down and express our gratitude to the One who made us, we enrich our own lives and the lives of those around us. That's why thanksgiving should become a habit, a regular part of our daily routines. God has blessed us beyond measure, and we owe Him everything, including our eternal praise.

God's Word makes it clear: a wise heart is a thankful heart. Period. We are to worship God, in part, by the genuine gratitude we feel in our hearts for the marvelous blessings that our Creator has bestowed upon us. Yet even the most saintly among us must endure periods of bitterness, fear, doubt, and regret. Why?

> God is worthy of our praise and is pleased when we come before Him with thanksgiving.
>
> Shirley Dobson

Because we are imperfect human beings who are incapable of perfect gratitude. Still, even on life's darker days, we must seek to cleanse our hearts of negative emotions and fill them, instead, with praise, with love, with hope, and with thanksgiving. To do otherwise is to be unfair to ourselves, to our loved ones, and to our God.

Have you established the habit of thanking God early and often? Do you appreciate the gifts that your Heavenly Father has given you? And, do you demonstrate your gratitude by being a faithful steward of the gifts and talents that you have received from your Creator? You most certainly should be thankful. After all, when you stop to think about it, God has given you more blessings than you can count. So the question of the day is this: will you thank your Heavenly Father . . . or will you spend your time and energy doing other things?

God is always listening—are you willing to say thanks? It's up to you, and the next move is yours.

I am to praise God for all things, regardless of where they seem to originate. Doing this is the key to receiving the blessings of God. Praise will wash away my resentments.

Catherine Marshall

It is always possible to be thankful for what is given rather than to complain about what is not given. One or the other becomes a habit of life.

Elisabeth Elliot

The act of thanksgiving is a demonstration of the fact that you are going to trust and believe God.

Kay Arthur

Therefore as you have received Christ Jesus the Lord, walk in Him, rooted and built up in Him and established in the faith, just as you were taught, and overflowing with thankfulness.

Colossians 2:6-7 Holman CSB

And let the peace of the Messiah, to which you were also called in one body, control your hearts. Be thankful.

Colossians 3:15 Holman CSB

Enter into His gates with thanksgiving, and into His courts with praise. Be thankful to Him, and bless His name. For the LORD is good; His mercy is everlasting, and His truth endures to all generations.

Psalm 100:4-5 NKJV

Thanks be to God for His indescribable gift.

2 Corinthians 9:15 Holman CSB

For More Thoughts About Praise and Thanksgiving,
Please Turn to Page 152

MY VALUES

	CHECK ONE:	
	YES	NO

I will not take my blessings for granted.

I will remain humble as I praise God and thank Him for His gifts.

I will not only thank God for His gifts, I will use those gifts as one way of honoring Him.

I expect God's continued blessings on my family.

My Prayer

Lord, let me be a thankful Christian. Your blessings are priceless and eternal. I praise You, Lord, for Your gifts and, most of all, for Your Son. Your love endures forever. I will offer You my heartfelt thanksgiving this day and throughout all eternity.

Amen

What I Can Do

_____

_____

_____

_____

_____

_____

_____

_____

_____

_____

_____

_____

_____

_____

_____

_____

_____

_____

_____

_____

_____

SIGN ON!

IF YOU AGREE TO THE ABOVE PLANS, PLEASE SIGN YOUR NAME.

FORMING THE HABIT OF . . .

Service

Worship the Lord your God and . . .
serve Him only.

Matthew 4:10 Holman CSB

Serving God can be habit-forming . . . and it's a habit that all Christians should acquire. Yet serving God isn't always our first priority. We live in a world that glorifies power, prestige, fame, and money. Yet the words of Jesus teach us that the most esteemed men and women are not the widely acclaimed leaders of society; the most esteemed among us are the humble servants of society.

When we experience success, it's easy to puff out our chests and proclaim, "I did that!" But it's wrong. Whatever "it" is, God did it, and He deserves the credit. As Christians, we have been refashioned and saved by Jesus Christ, and that salvation came not because of our own good works but because of God's grace.

> Through our service to others, God wants to influence our world for Him.
>
> Vonette Bright

Dietrich Bonhoeffer was correct when he observed, "It is very easy to overestimate the importance of our own achievements in comparison with what we owe others." In other words, reality breeds humility.

Are you willing to become a humble servant for Christ? Are you willing to pitch in and make the world a better place, or are you determined to keep all your blessings to yourself? The answer to these questions will determine the quantity and the quality of the service you render to God—and to His children.

Today, you may feel the temptation to take more than you give. You may be tempted to withhold your generosity. Or you may be tempted to build yourself up in the eyes of your friends. Resist these temptations. Instead, serve your friends quietly and without fanfare. Find a need and fill it . . . humbly. Lend a helping hand . . . anonymously. Share a word of kindness . . . with quiet sincerity. As you go about your daily activities, remember that the Savior of all humanity made Himself a servant, and you, as His follower, must do no less.

So many times we say that we can't serve God because we aren't whatever is needed. We're not talented enough or smart enough or whatever. But if you are in covenant with Jesus Christ, He is responsible for covering your weaknesses, for being your strength. He will give you His abilities for your disabilities!

Kay Arthur

God will open up places of service for you as He sees you are ready. Meanwhile, study the Bible and give yourself a chance to grow.

Warren Wiersbe

If you aren't serving, you're just existing, because life is meant for ministry.

Rick Warren

In the very place where God has put us, whatever its limitations, whatever kind of work it may be, we may indeed serve the Lord Christ.

Elisabeth Elliot

We must do the works of Him who sent Me while it is day. Night is coming when no one can work.

John 9:4 Holman CSB

If they serve Him obediently, they will end their days in prosperity and their years in happiness.

Job 36:11 Holman CSB

Serve the LORD with gladness.

Psalm 100:2 Holman CSB

A person should consider us in this way: as servants of Christ and managers of God's mysteries. In this regard, it is expected of managers that each one be found faithful.

1 Corinthians 4:1-2 Holman CSB

For More Thoughts About Service, Please Turn to Page 150

MY VALUES

	CHECK ONE:	
	YES	NO

Christ was a humble servant, and I value the importance of following His example.

_____ _____

I understand that greatness in God's kingdom relates to service, not status.

_____ _____

I will be proactive in my search to find ways to help others.

_____ _____

My Prayer

Dear Lord, in weak moments, I seek to build myself up by placing myself ahead of others. But Your commandment, Father, is that I become a humble servant to those who need my encouragement, my help, and my love. Create in me a servant's heart. And, let me be a woman who follows in the footsteps of Your Son Jesus who taught us by example that to be great in Your eyes, Lord, is to serve others humbly, faithfully, and lovingly.
Amen

What I Can Do

SIGN ON!

IF YOU AGREE TO THE ABOVE PLANS, PLEASE SIGN YOUR NAME.

FORMING THE HABIT OF . . .

Sharing God's Love

For God loved the world in this way: He gave His only Son, so that everyone who believes in Him will not perish but have eternal life.

John 3:16 Holman CSB

Have you formed the habit of accepting and sharing God's love? Hopefully so. After all, God's love for you is bigger and better than you can imagine. In fact, God's love is far too big to comprehend (in this lifetime). But this much we do know: God loves you so much that He sent His Son Jesus to come to this earth and to die for you. And, when you accepted Jesus into your heart, God gave you a gift that is more precious than gold: the gift of eternal life. Now, precisely because you are a wondrous creation treasured by God, a question presents itself: What will you do in response to God's love? Will you ignore it or embrace it? Will you return it or neglect it? Will you receive it and share it . . . or not? The answer to these simple questions will determine the level of your faith and the quality of your life.

> There are many timid souls whom we jostle morning and evening as we pass them by; but if only the kind word were spoken they might become fully persuaded.
>
> Fanny Crosby

When you form the habit of embracing God's love day in and day out, you feel differently about yourself, your neighbors, and your world. When you embrace God's love, you share His message and you obey His commandments.

When you accept the Father's gift of grace, you are blessed here on earth and throughout all eternity. So do yourself a favor right now: accept God's love with open arms and welcome His Son Jesus into your heart.

Corrie ten Boom observed, "We must mirror God's love in the midst of a world full of hatred. We are the mirrors of God's love, so we may show Jesus by our lives." And her words most certainly apply to Christian family, including yours.

God's heart is overflowing with love for you and yours. Accept that love. Return that love. Respect that love. And share that love. Today.

...God loves these people, too, just because they're unattractive or warped in their thinking doesn't mean the Lord doesn't love them.

Ruth Bell Graham

As God's children, we are the recipients of lavish love—a love that motivates us to keep trusting even when we have no idea what God is doing.

Beth Moore

Every tiny bit of my life that has value I owe to the redemption of Jesus Christ. Am I doing anything to enable Him to bring His redemption into evident reality in the lives of others?

Oswald Chambers

Whoever is wise will observe these things, and they will understand the lovingkindness of the LORD.

Psalm 107:43 NKJV

Sanctify the Lord God in your hearts: and be ready always to give an answer to every man that asketh you a reason of the hope that is in you . . . .

1 Peter 3:15 KJV

For the LORD is good, and His love is eternal; His faithfulness endures through all generations.

Psalm 100:5 Holman CSB

You are the light of the world. A city that is set on a hill cannot be hidden. Nor do they light a lamp and put it under a basket, but on a lampstand, and it gives light to all who are in the house. Let your light so shine before men, that they may see your good works and glorify your Father in heaven.

Matthew 5:14–16 NKJV

For More Thoughts About Love, Please Turn to Page 154

MY VALUES

	CHECK ONE:	
	YES	NO

I know that God loves me.
_____   _____

I understand the importance of a loving
relationship with God by spending time with Him.
_____   _____

I understand the importance of sharing God's love
with my family and friends.
_____   _____

My Prayer

Dear Lord, Your Word teaches us that You are love.
I will love You, Father, and I will share Your love
with my family and friends, today and forever.
Amen

What I Can Do

_____

SIGN ON!

IF YOU AGREE TO THE ABOVE PLANS, PLEASE SIGN YOUR NAME.

PART 2

Your
PHYSICAL
HEALTH

*Life is a gift—health must be earned.
We earn good health by cultivating
healthy habits.*

FORMING THE HABIT OF . . .

Sensible Exercise

*Therefore, brothers, by the mercies of God,
I urge you to present your bodies as a living
sacrifice, holy and pleasing to God;
this is your spiritual worship.*
Romans 12:1 Holman CSB

Are you shaping up or spreading out? Do you exercise regularly, or do you spend most of your time on the couch with a potato chip in one hand and a clicker in the other? Are you and your loved ones choosing to treat your bodies like temples—or not? How you answer these questions will help determine how long you live and how well you live.

Physical fitness is a habit, a habit that requires discipline—it's as simple as that. But here's the catch: understanding the need for discipline is easy, yet leading a disciplined life can be hard. Why? Because it's usually more fun to eat a second piece of cake than it is to jog a second lap around the track. Nonetheless, as we survey the second helpings that all too often find their way onto our plates, we should consider this: as Christians, we are instructed to lead disciplined lives, and when we behave in undisciplined ways, we are living outside of God's will.

> Eat to live, and not live to eat.
> Poor Richard's Almanac

We live in a world in which leisure is glorified and consumption is commercialized. But God has other plans. He did not create us for lives of gluttony or laziness; He created us for far greater things.

God has a plan for every aspect of your life, and His plan includes provisions for your physical health—and that means regular, sensible exercise. How much exercise is right for you? That's a decision that you should make in consultation with your physician. But make no mistake: if you sincerely desire to be a thoughtful caretaker of the body that God has given you, exercise is important.

Once you begin a regular exercise program, you'll discover that the benefits to you are not only physical but also psychological. Regular exercise allows you to build your muscles while you're clearing your head and lifting your spirits.

So, if you or your loved ones have been taking your bodies for granted, today is a wonderful day to change. You can start slowly, perhaps with a brisk walk around the block. As your stamina begins to build, so, too, will your sense of satisfaction. And, you'll be comforted by knowledge that you've done your part to protect and preserve the precious body that God has entrusted to your care.

Most people I know either love exercise and do it excessively, or they hate it and avoid it completely; yet consistent exercise is one of the keys to good health.

John Maxwell

Laughter is jogging for the insides. It increases heart rate and circulation, stimulates the immune system, and improves the muscle tone of the abdomen.

Barbara Johnson

Making up a string of excuses is usually harder than doing the work.

Marie T. Freeman

Don't you know that you are God's sanctuary and that the Spirit of God lives in you?

1 Corinthians 3:16 Holman CSB

For You formed my inward parts; You covered me in my mother's womb. I will praise You, for I am fearfully and wonderfully made; Marvelous are Your works.

Psalm 139:13-14 NKJV

Do you not know that your body is a sanctuary of the Holy Spirit who is in you, whom you have from God? You are not your own, for you were bought at a price; therefore glorify God in your body.

1 Corinthians 6:19-20 Holman CSB

MY VALUES

	CHECK ONE:	
	YES	NO

I understand the importance of sensible exercise.

I strive to make exercise enjoyable.

I understand that I and every member of my family should be engaged in a program of regular physical exercise.

My Prayer

Dear Lord, my body is, indeed, a priceless gift from You. Help me treat my body with care.
Amen

Never mind what others do; do better than yourself.
Beat your own record from day to day, and you are a success.
William Boetcker

What I Can Do

SIGN ON!

IF YOU AGREE TO THE ABOVE PLANS, PLEASE SIGN YOUR NAME.

FORMING THE HABIT OF . . .

Maintaining a Healthy Diet

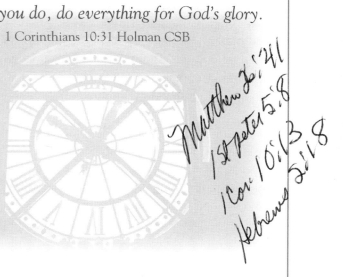

Therefore, whether you eat or drink, or whatever you do, do everything for God's glory.

1 Corinthians 10:31 Holman CSB

Matthew 26:41

1st Peter 5:8

1 Cor 10:13

Hebrews 2:18

Eating unhealthy foods is habit-forming. And if you have acquired the unfortunate habit of eating unhealthy foods, then God wants you to start making changes today.

Take a few minutes to think about your eating habits. Do you gobble down snack foods while watching television? If so, stop. Do you drink high calorie soft drinks or feast on unhealthy snacks like potato chips or candy? If so, you're doing yourself a disservice. Do you delight in high fat, high calorie foods that taste good for a few seconds but accumulate on your waistline for years? Do you load up your plate until food falls off the edge? And then do you feel obligated to eat every last bite? If so, it's time to think long and hard about the serious consequences of indulging in such unhealthy habits.

> Failure is the path of least persistence.
>
> Anonymous

Poor eating habits are easy to make and hard to break, but break them you must. Otherwise, you'll be disobeying God's commandments while causing yourself great harm.

Maintaining a healthy lifestyle is a journey, not a destination, and that journey requires discipline. But rest assured that if you and your loved ones are willing to make the step-by-step journey toward a healthier diet, God is taking careful note of your progress . . . and He's quietly urging you to take the next step.

It's not that some people have willpower and some don't.
It's that some people are ready to change and others are not.

James Gordon, M.D.

A Christian should no more defile his body than a Jew would defile the temple.

Warren Wiersbe

Always rise from the table with an appetite, and you will never sit down without one.

William Penn

We should take twice as long to eat half as much.

Anonymous

But I discipline my body and bring it into subjection, lest, when I have preached to others, I myself should become disqualified.

1 Corinthians 9:27 NKJV

The LORD is the strength of my life.

Psalm 27:1 KJV

I beseech you therefore, brethren, by the mercies of God, that you present your bodies a living sacrifice, holy, acceptable to God, which is your reasonable service. And do not be conformed to this world, but be transformed by the renewing of your mind, that you may prove what is that good and acceptable and perfect will of God.

Romans 12:1-2 NKJV

MY VALUES

I understand that my body is a priceless gift from God.

_____   _____

I know that I should treat my body with the utmost care.

_____   _____

I understand the importance of eating healthy foods.

_____   _____

I understand the need to be moderate, not gluttonous.

_____   _____

My Prayer

Dear Lord, You teach us that we should treat our bodies as temples. Keep us mindful that the foods we eat are important to our health, and that if we are to treat our bodies with respect, we should eat healthy foods in sensible amounts.
Amen

What I Can Do

SIGN ON!

IF YOU AGREE TO THE ABOVE PLANS, PLEASE SIGN YOUR NAME.

FORMING THE HABIT OF . . .

Observing the Sabbath

Remember the Sabbath day, to keep it holy.

Exodus 20:8 NKJV

When God gave Moses the Ten Commandments, it became perfectly clear that our Heavenly Father intends for His children to make the Sabbath a holy day, a day for worship, for contemplation, for fellowship, and for rest. Yet we live in a seven-day-a-week world, a world that all too often treats Sunday as a bonus shopping day or a regular workday. But the Lord's day deserves to be respected by those who choose to follow the Son of God.

You and your family members will face powerful temptations, temptations to rush through Sunday services and then get on with "business as usual." The world wants you to make Sunday a time for shopping, a time for working, a time for rushing from place to place with scarcely a moment to spare. But God wants you to make the Sabbath a special day—and that's precisely what you should want for you and your family.

> Life is strenuous. See that your clock does not run down.
>
> Mrs. Charles E. Cowman

How does your family observe the Lord's day? When church is over, do you treat Sunday like any other day of the week? If so, it's time to think long and hard about your family's schedule and your family's priorities.

Whenever we ignore God's commandments, we pay a price. So if you've been treating Sunday as just another day, it's time to break that habit. When Sunday rolls around, don't try to fill every spare moment. Take time to worship and to rest . . . Father's orders!

Jesus taught us by example to get out of the rat race and recharge our batteries.

Barbara Johnson

Jesus gives us the ultimate rest, the confidence we need, to escape the frustration and chaos of the world around us.

Billy Graham

It is what Jesus is, not what we are, that gives rest to the soul. If we really want to overcome Satan and have peace with God, we must "fix our eyes on Jesus." Let his death, his suffering, his glories, and his intercession be fresh on your mind.

C. H. Spurgeon

God has promised to give you all of eternity. The least you can do is give Him one day a week in return.

Marie T. Freeman

THE TEN COMMANDMENTS

Then God spoke all these words: I am the LORD your God, who brought you out of the land of Egypt, out of the place of slavery. Do not have other gods besides Me. Do not make an idol for yourself, whether in the shape of anything in the heavens above or on the earth below or in the waters under the earth. You must not bow down to them or worship them; for I, the LORD your God, am a jealous God, punishing the children for the fathers' sin, to the third and fourth [generations] of those who hate Me, but showing faithful love to a thousand [generations] of those who love Me and keep My commands. Do not misuse the name of the LORD your God, because the LORD will punish anyone who misuses His name. Remember to dedicate the Sabbath day: You are to labor six days and do all your work, but the seventh day is a Sabbath to the LORD your God. You must not do any work—you, your son or daughter, your male or female slave, your livestock, or the foreigner who is within your gates. For the LORD made the heavens and the earth, the sea, and everything in them in six days; then He rested on the seventh day. Therefore the LORD blessed the Sabbath day and declared it holy. Honor your father and your mother so that you may have a long life in the land that the LORD your God is giving you. Do not murder. Do not commit adultery. Do not steal. Do not give false testimony against your neighbor. Do not covet your neighbor's house. Do not covet your neighbor's wife, his male or female slave, his ox or donkey, or anything that belongs to your neighbor.

Exodus 20:1-17 HOLMAN CSB

MY VALUES

	CHECK ONE:	
	YES	NO

I respect God's commandment that one day
a week should be His.

_____ _____

I believe that Sunday is a special day, and
I treat it that way.

_____ _____

I reserve Sunday as a time of worship, praise,
reflection, fellowship, and rest.

_____ _____

My Prayer

Lord, when I am ill or weak or troubled,
You heal me. Renew me, Father, and let me trust
Your will for my life. Let me welcome Your unending
love and Your healing touch, now and forever.
Amen

What I Can Do

_____

_____

_____

_____

_____

_____

_____

_____

_____

_____

_____

_____

_____

_____

_____

_____

_____

SIGN ON!

_____

IF YOU AGREE TO THE ABOVE PLANS, PLEASE SIGN YOUR NAME.

DAY 13

FORMING THE HABIT OF . . .

Getting Enough Sleep

But those who wait on the LORD Shall renew their strength; They shall mount up with wings like eagles, They shall run and not be weary, They shall walk and not faint.

Isaiah 40:31 NKJV

Are you in the habit of going to bed at an early hour so that you can get about eight hours' sleep each night? Or do you stay up late trying to "entertain" yourself when you should be sleeping? If you're not getting enough rest, then you're asking for trouble, and lots of it.

God intends that all His children (including you) lead joyous lives filled with abundance and peace. But sometimes, abundance and peace seem very far away. It is during these darker moments that we must turn to God for renewal and for strength—and when we do, He will restore our physical and emotional strength.

Physical exhaustion is God's way of telling us to slow down. God expects us to work hard, of course, but He also intends for us to rest. When we fail to take the rest that we need, we do a disservice to ourselves and to our families.

> If you can't sleep, don't count sheep; talk to the Shepherd.
>
> Anonymous

We live in a world that tempts us to stay up late—very late. But too much late-night TV, combined with too little sleep, is a prescription for exhaustion—and it's a prescription that you should avoid. Otherwise, you'll find yourself running short of energy, short on patience, and short on perspective.

Are your physical or spiritual batteries running low? Is your energy on the wane? Are your emotions frayed? If so, it's time to turn your thoughts and your prayers to God. And when you're finished, it's probably time to turn off the lights and go to bed!

Come, come, come unto Me, weary and sore distressed; come, come, come unto Me, come unto Me and rest.

Fanny Crosby

Life is strenuous. See that your clock does not run down.

Mrs. Charles E. Cowman

Prescription for a happier and healthier life: resolve to slow down your pace; learn to say no gracefully; resist the temptation to chase after more pleasure, more hobbies, and more social entanglements.

James Dobson

Taking care of yourself physically really helps emotionally. People who get a lot of sleep, who do the things that relieve stress, can withstand a lot of stress.

Laura Bush

But may the God of all grace, who called us to His eternal glory by Christ Jesus, after you have suffered a while, perfect, establish, strengthen, and settle you.

1 Peter 5:10 NKJV

Come to Me, all you who labor and are heavy laden, and I will give you rest. Take My yoke upon you and learn from Me, for I am gentle and lowly in heart, and you will find rest for your souls. For My yoke is easy and My burden is light.

Matthew 11:28-30 NKJV

You are being renewed in the spirit of your minds; you put on the new man, the one created according to God's likeness in righteousness and purity of the truth.

Ephesians 4:23-24 Holman CSB

Rest in God alone, my soul, for my hope comes from Him.

Psalm 62:5 Holman CSB

MY VALUES

I understand the need for adequate rest.

I plan my activities in order that I get to be in at an hour that allows for sufficient sleep.

I understand that I feel better and function better when I'm rested.

CHECK ONE:	
YES	NO
___	___
___	___
___	___

My Prayer

Dear Lord, when I'm tired, give me the wisdom to do the smart thing: give me the wisdom to put my head on my pillow and rest!
Amen

If you're sick and tired of feeling sick and tired,
turn off the TV and go to bed.
Marie T. Freeman

What I Can Do

_____
_____
_____
_____
_____
_____
_____
_____
_____
_____
_____
_____
_____
_____
_____
_____
_____
_____
_____
_____
_____
_____

SIGN ON!

_____

IF YOU AGREE TO THE ABOVE PLANS, PLEASE SIGN YOUR NAME.

PART 3

Your
EMOTIONAL
HEALTH

Emotions are contagious.
You should strive to make certain that
the emotions you share with your family
and friends are healthy emotions.

FORMING THE HABIT OF . . .

Thinking Clearly

Finally brothers, whatever is true, whatever is honorable, whatever is just, whatever is pure, whatever is lovely, whatever is commendable— if there is any moral excellence and if there is any praise—dwell on these things.

Philippians 4:8 Holman CSB

How will you direct your thoughts today? Will you form the habit of thinking positive thoughts about your life and your future? Will you be a woman whose hopes and dreams are alive and well? Will you put a smile on your face and a song in your heart? Hopefully so. But here's a word of warning: sometimes, when pessimism, frustration, or doubt threaten to hijack your emotions, you won't feel much like celebrating. That's why you must always strive to keep your thoughts headed in the right direction.

Your thoughts have the power to lift you up or to drag you down; they have the power to energize you or deplete you, to inspire you to greater accomplishments or to make those accomplishments impossible.

> It is the thoughts and intents of the heart that shape a person's life.
>
> John Eldredge

What kind of attitude will you select today? Will you obey the words of Philippians 4:7-8 by dwelling upon those things that are "honorable, just, and pure"? Or will you allow yourself to be swayed by the negativity that seems to dominate our troubled world?

What kind of attitude will you select today? Will you obey the words of Philippians 4:7-8 by dwelling upon those things that are "true and honorable and right?" Or will you allow yourself to be swayed by the negativity that seems to dominate our troubled world?

God intends that you experience joy and abundance, but He will not force His joy upon you; you must claim it for yourself. It's up to you to celebrate the life that God has given you by focusing your mind upon "things that are excellent and worthy of praise." So today, spend more time thinking about your blessings and less time fretting about your hardships. Then, take time to thank the Giver of all things good for gifts that are, in truth, far too numerous to count.

As we have by faith said no to sin, so we should by faith say yes to God and set our minds on things above, where Christ is seated in the heavenlies.

Vonette Bright

No more imperfect thoughts. No more sad memories. No more ignorance. My redeemed body will have a redeemed mind. Grant me a foretaste of that perfect mind as you mirror your thoughts in me today.

Joni Eareckson Tada

The things we think are the things that feed our souls. If we think on pure and lovely things, we shall grow pure and lovely like them; and the converse is equally true.

Hannah Whitall Smith

Your thoughts are the determining factor as to whose mold you are conformed to. Control your thoughts and you control the direction of your life.

Charles Stanley

Set your minds on what is above, not on what is on the earth.

Colossians 3:2 Holman CSB

For God has not given us a spirit of fearfulness, but one of power, love, and sound judgment.

2 Timothy 1:7 Holman CSB

I, the LORD, examine the mind, I test the heart to give to each according to his way, according to what his actions deserve.

Jeremiah 17:10 Holman CSB

Brothers, don't be childish in your thinking, but be infants in evil and adult in your thinking.

1 Corinthians 14:20 Holman CSB

For More Thoughts About Attitude, Please Turn to Page 160

MY VALUES

CHECK ONE:
YES   NO

I understand the importance of directing my thoughts in positive directions.

I believe that emotions are contagious, so I try to associate with people who are upbeat, optimistic, and encouraging.

I trust that when I dwell on positive thoughts and when I focus on God's blessings, I will feel better about myself and my circumstances.

My Prayer

Dear Lord, keep my thoughts focused on Your love,
Your power, Your promises, and Your Son.
When I am worried, I will turn to You for comfort;
when I am weak, I will turn to You for strength;
when I am troubled, I will turn to You for patience
and perspective. Help me guard my thoughts,
Father, so that I may honor You today
and every day that I live.
Amen

What I Can Do

_____

SIGN ON!

IF YOU AGREE TO THE ABOVE PLANS, PLEASE SIGN YOUR NAME.

FORMING THE HABIT OF . . .

Encouraging Others

I want their hearts to be encouraged and joined together in love, so that they may have all the riches of assured understanding, and have the knowledge of God's mystery—Christ.

Colossians 2:2 Holman CSB

Life is a team sport, and all of us need occasional pats on the back from our teammates. This world can be a difficult place, a place where many of our friends and family members are troubled by the challenges of everyday life. And since we cannot always be certain who needs our help, we should strive to speak helpful words to all who cross our paths.

In his letter to the Ephesians, Paul writes, "Do not let any unwholesome talk come out of your mouths, but only what is helpful for building others up according to their needs, that it may benefit those who listen" (4:29 NIV). This passage reminds us that, as Christians, we are instructed to choose our words carefully so as to build others up through wholesome, honest encouragement. How can we build others up? By celebrating their victories and their accomplishments. As the old saying goes, "When someone does something good, applaud—you'll make two people happy."

Genuine encouragement should never be confused with pity. God intends for His children to lead lives of abundance, joy, celebration, and praise—not lives of self-pity or regret. So we must guard ourselves against hosting (or joining) the "pity parties" that so often accompany difficult times. Instead, we must encourage each other to have faith—first in God and His only begotten Son—and then in our own abilities to use the talents God has given us for the furtherance of His kingdom and for the betterment of our own lives.

> Overcoming discouragement is simply a matter of taking away the DIS and adding the EN.
>
> Barbara Johnson

As a faithful follower of Jesus, you have every reason to be hopeful, and you have every reason to share your hopes with others. When you do, you will discover that hope, like other human emotions, is contagious. So do the world (and yourself) a favor: Look for the good in others and celebrate the good that you find. When you do, you'll be a powerful force of encouragement to your friends and family . . . and a worthy servant to your God.

One of the ways God refills us after failure is through the blessing of Christian fellowship. Just experiencing the joy of simple activities shared with other children of God can have a healing effect on us.

Anne Graham Lotz

The glory of friendship is not the outstretched hand, or the kindly smile, or the joy of companionship. It is the spiritual inspiration that comes to one when he discovers that someone else believes in him and is willing to trust him with his friendship.

Corrie ten Boom

Carry one another's burdens; in this way you will fulfill the law of Christ.

Galatians 6:2 Holman CSB

And let us be concerned about one another in order to promote love and good works.

Hebrews 10:24 Holman CSB

But encourage each other daily, while it is still called today, so that none of you is hardened by sin's deception.

Hebrews 3:13 Holman CSB

Iron sharpens iron, and one man sharpens another.

Proverbs 27:17 Holman CSB

For More Thoughts About Encouragement, Please Turn to Page 158

MY VALUES

	CHECK ONE:	
	YES	NO

I believe that God wants me to encourage other people.

_____   _____

I carefully think about the words I speak so that every word might be a "gift of encouragement" to others.

_____   _____

I believe that my words reflect my heart. I will guard my heart so that my words will be pleasing to God.

_____   _____

My Prayer

Make me sensitive, O Lord, to the many gifts of encouragement I receive each day. And, let me be a source of encouragement to all who cross my path. The Bible tells of Your servant Barnabas. Like Barnabas, I, too, want to be an encourager to my family and friends so that I might do Your work and share Your love.
Amen

What I Can Do

_____
_____
_____
_____
_____
_____
_____
_____
_____
_____
_____
_____
_____
_____
_____
_____
_____
_____
_____
_____

SIGN ON!

_____

IF YOU AGREE TO THE ABOVE PLANS, PLEASE SIGN YOUR NAME.

FORMING THE HABIT OF . . .

*Rejoice in hope; be patient in affliction;
be persistent in prayer.*
Romans 12:12 Holman CSB

The dictionary defines the word *patience* as "the ability to be calm, tolerant, and understanding." If you've acquired the habit of being calm, tolerant, and understanding even when circumstances are difficult, then you can skip the rest of this page. But, if you're like most of us, you'd better keep reading.

For most of us, patience is a hard thing to master. Why? Because we have lots of things we want, and we know precisely when we want them: NOW (if not sooner). But our Father in heaven has other ideas; the Bible teaches that we must learn to wait patiently for the things that God has in store for us, even when waiting is difficult.

We live in an imperfect world inhabited by imperfect people. Sometimes, we inherit troubles from others, and sometimes we create troubles for ourselves. On other occasions, we see other people "moving ahead" in the world, and we want to move ahead with them. So we become impatient with ourselves, with our circumstances, and even with our Creator.

> Waiting is an essential part of spiritual discipline. It can be the ultimate test of faith.
>
> Anne Graham Lotz

Psalm 37:7 commands us to "rest in the LORD, and wait patiently for Him" (NKJV). But, for most of us, waiting patiently for Him is hard. We are fallible human beings who seek solutions to our problems today, not tomorrow. Still, God instructs us to wait patiently for His plans to unfold, and that's exactly what we should do.

Sometimes, patience is the price we pay for being responsible adults, and that's as it should be. After all, think how patient our Heavenly Father has been with us. So the next time you find yourself drumming your fingers as you wait for a quick resolution to the challenges of everyday living, take a deep breath and ask God for patience. Be still before your Heavenly Father and trust His timetable: it's the peaceful way to live.

Waiting means going about our assigned tasks, confident that God will provide the meaning and the conclusions.

Eugene Peterson

No matter what we are going through, no matter how long the waiting for answers, of one thing we may be sure. God is faithful. He keeps His promises. What He starts, He finishes . . . including His perfect work in us.

Gloria Gaither

To receive the blessing we need, we must believe and keep on believing, and we must also wait and keep on waiting. We need to wait in prayer, wait with our Bibles open as we confess his promises, wait in joyful praise and worship of the God who will never forget our case, and wait as we continue serving others in his name.

Jim Cymbala

Be gentle to everyone, able to teach, and patient.

2 Timothy 2:23 Holman CSB

Now we exhort you, brethren, warn those who are unruly, comfort the fainthearted, uphold the weak, be patient with all.

1 Thessalonians 5:14 NKJV

Love is patient; love is kind.

1 Corinthians 13:4 Holman CSB

A patient spirit is better than a proud spirit.

Ecclesiastes 7:8 Holman CSB

For More Thoughts About Patience, Please Turn to Page 164

MY VALUES

	CHECK ONE:
	YES NO

I take seriously the Bible's instructions to
be patient.

_____ _____

I believe that patience is not idle waiting but
that it is an activity that requires me to watch
and wait for God to lead me.

_____ _____

Even when I don't understand the circumstances
that confront me, I strive to wait patiently while
serving the Lord.

_____ _____

My Prayer

*Lord, make me a woman of patience. When I am
hurried, give me peace. When I am frustrated, give me
perspective. When I am angry, let me turn my heart to
You. Today, let me be a patient Christian, Dear Lord,
as I trust in You and in Your master plan for my life.
Amen*

What I Can Do

_____

_____

_____

_____

_____

_____

_____

_____

_____

_____

_____

_____

_____

_____

_____

_____

_____

_____

SIGN ON!

_____

IF YOU AGREE TO THE ABOVE PLANS, PLEASE SIGN YOUR NAME.

FORMING THE HABIT OF . . .

Celebrating Life

This is the day the LORD has made;
we will rejoice and be glad in it.
Psalm 118:24 NKJV

Today is a non-renewable resource—once it's gone, it's gone forever. Our responsibility, as thoughtful believers, is to use this day in the service of God's will and in the service of His people. When we do so, we enrich our own lives and the lives of those whom we love.

God has richly blessed us, and He wants you to rejoice in His gifts. That's why this day—and each day that follows—should be a time of prayer and celebration as we consider the Good News of God's free gift: salvation through Jesus Christ.

Oswald Chambers correctly observed, "Joy is the great note all throughout the Bible." E. Stanley Jones echoed that thought when he wrote "Christ and joy go together." But, even the most dedicated Christians can, on occasion, forget to celebrate each day for what it is: a priceless gift from God.

> Life is a glorious opportunity.
> Billy Graham

What do you expect from the day ahead? Are you expecting God to do wonderful things, or are you living beneath a cloud of apprehension and doubt? The familiar words of Psalm 118:24 remind us of a profound yet simple truth: "This is the day which the LORD hath made" (KJV). Our duty, as believers, is to rejoice in God's marvelous creation.

Today, celebrate the life that God has given you. Today, put a smile on your face, kind words on your lips, and a song in your heart. Be generous with your praise and free with your encouragement. And then, when you have celebrated life to the fullest, invite your friends to do likewise. After all, this is God's day, and He has given us clear instructions for its use. We are commanded to rejoice and be glad. So, with no further ado, let the celebration begin . . .

If you can forgive the person you were, accept the person you are, and believe in the person you will become, you are headed for joy. So celebrate your life.

Barbara Johnson

Some of us seem so anxious about avoiding hell that we forget to celebrate our journey toward heaven.

Philip Yancey

The happiest people in the world are not those who have no problems, but the people who have learned to live with those things that are less than perfect.

James Dobson

Christ is the secret, the source, the substance, the center, and the circumference of all true and lasting gladness.

Mrs. Charles E. Cowman

David and the whole house of Israel were celebrating before the LORD.

2 Samuel 6:5 Holman CSB

Rejoice in the Lord always. I will say it again: Rejoice!

Philippians 4:4 Holman CSB

Their sorrow was turned into rejoicing and their mourning into a holiday. They were to be days of feasting, rejoicing, and of sending gifts to one another and the poor.

Esther 9:22 Holman CSB

At the dedication of the wall of Jerusalem, they sent for the Levites wherever they lived and brought them to Jerusalem to celebrate the joyous dedication with thanksgiving and singing accompanied by cymbals, harps, and lyres.

Nehemiah 12:27 Holman CSB

For More Thoughts About Celebrating Life, Please Turn to Page 162

MY VALUES

	CHECK ONE:	
	YES	NO

I understand that every day can and should be
a cause for celebration.

_____   _____

I will strive to worry less and trust God more.

_____   _____

I will share my enthusiasm with my family
members, with my friends, and with the world.

_____   _____

My Prayer

Lord God, You have given me so many reasons to
celebrate. The heavens proclaim Your handiwork,
and every star in the sky tells of Your power.
You sent Your Son to die for my sins, and You gave
me the gift of eternal life. Let me be mindful of all
my blessings, and let me celebrate You and
Your marvelous creation. Today is Your gift to me,
Lord. Let me use it to Your glory.
Amen

What I Can Do

SIGN ON!

IF YOU AGREE TO THE ABOVE PLANS. PLEASE SIGN YOUR NAME.

FORMING THE HABIT OF . . .

Discipline

No discipline seems enjoyable at the time, but painful. Later on, however, it yields the fruit of peace and righteousness to those who have been trained by it.

Hebrews 12:11 Holman CSB

Are you a self-disciplined person? If so, congratulations . . . if not, it's time to think long and hard about your values, your priorities, and your habits.

God's Word makes it clear that He doesn't reward laziness, misbehavior, or apathy. To the contrary, He expects believers (like you) to behave with dignity and discipline.

You live in a world where leisure is glorified and indifference is often glamorized—but God has bigger things in store for you. He did not create you for a life of mediocrity; He created you for far greater things. God has given you a unique assortment of talents and opportunities . . . and He expects you to use them. But beware: it is not always easy to cultivate those talents.

> The Bible calls for discipline and a recognition of authority. Children must learn this at home.
>
> Billy Graham

Sometimes, you must invest countless hours (or, in some cases, many years) honing your skills. And that's perfectly okay with God, because He understands that self-discipline is a blessing, not a burden.

When you pause to consider how much work needs to be done, you'll realize that self-discipline is not simply a proven way to get ahead, it's also an integral part of God's plan for your life. If you genuinely seek to be faithful stewards of your time, your talents, and your resources, you must adopt a disciplined approach to life. Otherwise, your talents may go unused and your resources may be squandered.

So, as you plan for your future, remember this: life's greatest rewards are unlikely to fall into your lap; to the contrary, your greatest accomplishments will probably require lots of work and plenty of self-discipline. And it's up to you to behave accordingly.

The alternative to discipline is disaster.

Vance Havner

If one examines the secret behind a championship football team, a magnificent orchestra, or a successful business, the principal ingredient is invariably discipline.

James Dobson

God cannot build character without our cooperation. If we resist Him, then He chastens us into submission. But, if we submit to Him, then He can accomplish His work. He is not satisfied with a halfway job. God wants a perfect work; He wants a finished product that is mature and complete.

Warren Wiersbe

As we seek to become disciples of Jesus Christ, we should never forget that the word *disciple* is directly related to the word *discipline*. To be a disciple of the Lord Jesus Christ is to know his discipline.

Dennis Swanberg

For this very reason, make every effort to supplement your faith with goodness, goodness with knowledge, knowledge with self-control, self-control with endurance, endurance with godliness.

2 Peter 1:5-6 Holman CSB

The one who follows instruction is on the path to life, but the one who rejects correction goes astray.

Proverbs 10:17 Holman CSB

I discipline my body and bring it under strict control, so that after preaching to others, I myself will not be disqualified.

1 Corinthians 9:27 Holman CSB

Therefore by their fruits you will know them.

Matthew 7:20 NKJV

For More Thoughts About Self-Discipline, Please Turn to Page 170

MY VALUES

	CHECK ONE:	
	YES	NO

I value the rewards of a disciplined lifestyle.

_____ _____

I understand the importance of disciplining myself emotionally, mentally, spiritually, and physically.

_____ _____

I believe that when I work hard, my work is usually rewarded.

_____ _____

My Prayer

Dear Lord, make me a woman of discipline and righteousness. Let my conduct show others what it means to be a faithful Christian, and let me follow Your will and Your Word, today and every day.
Amen

What I Can Do

_____

_____

_____

_____

_____

_____

_____

_____

_____

_____

_____

_____

_____

_____

_____

_____

_____

_____

_____

_____

SIGN ON!

IF YOU AGREE TO THE ABOVE PLANS, PLEASE SIGN YOUR NAME.

FORMING THE HABIT OF . . .

Worrying Less

(WHILE TRUSTING GOD MORE)

*Trust in the LORD with all your heart,
and do not rely on your own understanding;
think about Him in all your ways,
and He will guide you on the right paths.*

Proverbs 3:5-6 HOLMAN CSB

Have you acquired the habit of worrying about almost everything under the sun? If so, it's a habit you should break.

Even if you're a very faithful Christian, you may be plagued by occasional periods of discouragement and doubt. Even though you trust God's promise of salvation—even though you sincerely believe in God's love and protection—you may find yourself upset by the countless details of everyday life. Jesus understood your concerns when He spoke the reassuring words found in the 6th chapter of Matthew:

> "Therefore I say to you, do not worry about your life, what you will eat or what you will drink; nor about your body, what you will put on. Is not life more than food and the body more than clothing? Look at the birds of the air, for they neither sow nor reap nor gather into barns; yet your heavenly Father feeds them. Are you not of more value than they? Which of you by worrying can add one cubit to his stature? . . . Therefore do not worry about tomorrow, for tomorrow will worry about its own things. Sufficient for the day is its own trouble." (vv. 25-27, 34 NKJV)

> Never imagine that you can be a loser by trusting in God.
>
> C. H. Spurgeon

Where is the best place to take your worries? Take them to God. Take your troubles to Him; take your fears to Him; take your doubts to Him; take your weaknesses to Him; take your sorrows to Him . . . and leave them all there. Seek protection from the One who offers you eternal salvation; build your spiritual house upon the Rock that cannot be moved.

Perhaps you are concerned about your future, your relationships, or your finances. Or perhaps you are simply a "worrier" by nature. If so, choose to make Matthew 6 a regular part of your daily Bible reading. This beautiful passage will remind you that God still sits in His heaven and you are His beloved child. Then, perhaps, you will worry a little less and trust God a little more, and that's as it should be because God is trustworthy . . . and you are protected.

Worship and worry cannot live in the same heart; they are mutually exclusive.

Ruth Bell Graham

As God's children, we are the recipients of lavish love—a love that motivates us to keep trusting even when we have no idea what God is doing.

Beth Moore

Faith is nothing more or less than actively trusting God.

Catherine Marshall

We trust not because "a God" exists, but because this God exists.

C. S. Lewis

For the eyes of the LORD range throughout the earth to show Himself strong for those whose hearts are completely His.

2 Chronicles 16:9 HOLMAN CSB

He granted their request because they trusted in Him.

1 Chronicles 5:20 HOLMAN CSB

Let us hold fast the confession of our hope without wavering, for He who promised is faithful.

Hebrews 10:23 NKJV

The one who understands a matter finds success, and the one who trusts in the LORD will be happy.

Proverbs 16:20 HOLMAN CSB

For More Thoughts About Worry, Please Turn to Page 168

MY VALUES

I will trust God in every season of life, in good times and hard times.

I will use faith as an antidote to worry.

I will remember that God has been trustworthy in the past, so I will trust Him to protect me today.

I will trust God's Word, and I will expect Him to fulfill His promises.

CHECK ONE:

YES	NO
____	____
____	____
____	____
____	____

My Prayer

Dear Lord, even when I don't understand why things happen, I will trust You. Even when I am confused or worried, I will trust You. There are many things that I cannot do, Lord, and there are many things that I cannot understand. But one thing I can do is to trust You always. And I will.

Amen

What I Can Do

SIGN ON!

IF YOU AGREE TO THE ABOVE PLANS, PLEASE SIGN YOUR NAME.

FORMING THE HABIT OF . . .

Spiritual Growth

*For this reason also, since the day we heard
this, we haven't stopped praying for you.
We are asking that you may be filled with
the knowledge of His will in all wisdom and
spiritual understanding.*

Colossians 1:9 Holman CSB

The path to spiritual maturity unfolds day by day. Each day offers the opportunity to worship God, to ignore God, or to rebel against God. When we worship Him with our prayers, our words, our thoughts, and our actions, we are blessed by the richness of our relationship with the Father. But if we ignore God altogether or intentionally rebel against His commandments, we rob ourselves of His blessings.

If we study God's Word, if we obey His commandments, and if we live in the center of His will, we will not be "stagnant" believers; we will, instead, be growing Christians . . . and that's exactly what God wants for our lives.

Many of life's most important lessons are painful to learn, but spiritual growth need not take place only in times of adversity. We must seek to grow in our knowledge and love of the Lord in every season of life. Thankfully, God always stands at the door; whenever we are ready to reach out to Him, He will answer.

> One of the marks of Spiritual maturity is a consistent, Spirit-controlled life.
>
> Vonette Bright

In those quiet moments when we open our hearts to the Father, the One who made us keeps remaking us. He gives us direction, perspective, wisdom, and courage. And, the appropriate moment to accept those spiritual gifts is always the present one.

Are you as mature as you're ever going to be? Hopefully not! When it comes to your faith, God doesn't intend for you to become "fully grown," at least not in this lifetime. In fact, God still has important lessons that He intends to teach you. So ask yourself this: what lesson is God trying to teach me today? And then go about the business of learning it.

The Holy Spirit was given to guide us into all truth, but He doesn't do it all at once.

Elisabeth Elliot

You are either becoming more like Christ every day or you're becoming less like Him. There is no neutral position in the Lord.

Stormie Omartian

We look at our burdens and heavy loads, and we shrink from them. But, if we lift them and bind them about our hearts, they become wings, and on them we can rise and soar toward God.

Mrs. Charles E. Cowman

The key to contentment is to consider. Consider who you are and be satisfied with that. Consider what you have and be satisfied with that. Consider what God's doing and be satisfied with that.

Luci Swindoll

But grow in the grace and knowledge of our Lord and Savior Jesus Christ. To Him be the glory both now and to the day of eternity.

2 Peter 3:18 Holman CSB

I want their hearts to be encouraged and joined together in love, so that they may have all the riches of assured understanding, and have the knowledge of God's mystery—Christ.

Colossians 2:2 Holman CSB

Therefore, leaving the elementary message about the Messiah, let us go on to maturity.

Hebrews 6:1 Holman CSB

For You, O God, have tested us; You have refined us as silver is refined. You brought us into the net; You laid affliction on our backs. You have caused men to ride over our heads; we went through fire and through water; but You brought us out to rich fulfillment.

Psalm 66:10–12 NKJV

MY VALUES

	CHECK ONE:	
	YES	NO

I believe that the level of my spiritual maturity
has a direct impact, either positively or negatively,
on those around me.

— ——— ———

Since I believe that I still have "room to grow"
in my faith, gaining spiritual maturity remains
a priority for me.

— ——— ———

Since I feel that spiritual growth happens day by
day, I will live, worship, and pray accordingly.

— ——— ———

My Prayer

*Heavenly Father, I want to grow closer to You each
day. I know that obedience to Your will strengthens
my relationship with You, so help me to follow
Your commandments and obey Your Word today . . .
and every day of my life.
Amen*

What I Can Do

SIGN ON!

IF YOU AGREE TO THE ABOVE PLANS, PLEASE SIGN YOUR NAME.

FORMING THE HABIT OF . . .

Living Purposefully

*For it is God who is working among you
both the willing and the working
for His good purpose.*
Philippians 2:13 Holman CSB

L ife is best lived on purpose, not by accident: the sooner we discover what God intends for us to do with our lives, the better. But God's purposes aren't always clear to us. Sometimes we wander aimlessly in a wilderness of our own making. And sometimes, we struggle mightily against God in a vain effort to find success and happiness through our own means, not His.

Whenever we struggle against God's plans, we suffer. When we resist God's calling, our efforts bear little fruit. Our best strategy, therefore, is to seek God's wisdom and to follow Him wherever He chooses to lead. When we do so, we are blessed.

When we align ourselves with God's purposes, we avail ourselves of His power and His peace. But how can we know precisely what God's intentions are? The answer, of course, is that even the most well-intentioned believers face periods of uncertainty and doubt about the direction of their lives. So, too, will you.

When you arrive at one of life's inevitable crossroads, that is precisely the moment when you should turn your thoughts and prayers toward God. When you do, He will make Himself known to you in a time and manner of His choosing.

Are you earnestly seeking to discern God's purpose for your life? If so, these pages are intended as a reminder of several important facts: 1. God has a plan for your life; 2. If you seek

> Yesterday is just experience but tomorrow is glistening with purpose—and today is the channel leading from one to the other.
>
> Barbara Johnson

that plan sincerely and prayerfully, you will find it; 3. When you discover God's purpose for your life, you will experience abundance, peace, joy, and power—God's power. And that's the only kind of power that really matters.

If you want purpose and meaning and satisfaction and fulfillment and peace and hope and joy and abundant life that lasts forever, look to Jesus.

Anne Graham Lotz

It is important to set goals because if you do not have a plan, a goal, a direction, a purpose, and a focus, you are not going to accomplish anything for the glory of God.

Bill Bright

Great relief and satisfaction can come from seeking God's priorities for us in each season, discerning what is "best" in the midst of many noble opportunities, and pouring our most excellent energies into those things.

Beth Moore

Victory is the result of Christ's life lived out in the believer. It is important to see that victory, not defeat, is God's purpose for His children.

Corrie ten Boom

We know that all things work together for the good of those who love God: those who are called according to His purpose.

Romans 8:28 Holman CSB

I will instruct you and show you the way to go; with My eye on you, I will give counsel.

Psalm 32:8 Holman CSB

You reveal the path of life to me; in Your presence is abundant joy; in Your right hand are eternal pleasures.

Psalm 16:11 Holman CSB

Commit your activities to the LORD and your plans will be achieved.

Proverbs 16:3 Holman CSB

For More Thoughts About Living Purposefully,
Please Turn to Page 172

MY VALUES

	CHECK ONE:	
	YES	NO

I will seek to discover God's unfolding purpose for my life.

_____   _____

I will consult God on matters great and small.

_____   _____

I will pray about my plans for the future.

_____   _____

I will remain open to the opportunities and challenges that God places before me.

_____   _____

My Prayer

Dear Lord, You are the Creator of the universe, and I know that Your plan for my life is grander than I can imagine. Let Your purposes be my purposes, and let me trust in the assurance of Your promises.
Amen

What I Can Do

_____

SIGN ON!

_____

IF YOU AGREE TO THE ABOVE PLANS, PLEASE SIGN YOUR NAME.

More Thoughts About . . .

OBEDIENCE

The cross that Jesus commands you and me to carry is the cross of submissive obedience to the will of God, even when His will includes suffering and hardship and things we don't want to do.

Anne Graham Lotz

You may not always see immediate results, but all God wants is your obedience and faithfulness.

Vonette Bright

I don't always like His decisions, but when I choose to obey Him, the act of obedience still "counts" with Him even if I'm not thrilled about it.

Beth Moore

Trials and sufferings teach us to obey the Lord by faith, and we soon learn that obedience pays off in joyful ways.

Bill Bright

God uses broken things: broken soil and broken clouds to produce grain; broken grain to produce bread; broken bread to feed our bodies. He wants our stubbornness broken into humble obedience.

Vance Havner

Jesus is Victor. Calvary is the place of victory. Obedience is the pathway of victory. Bible study and prayer is the preparation for victory.

Corrie ten Boom

True faith commits us to obedience.

A. W. Tozer

Mary could not have dreamed all that would result from her faithful obedience. Likewise, you cannot possibly imagine all that God has in store for you when you trust him.

Henry Blackaby

Let us never suppose that obedience is impossible or that holiness is meant only for a select few. Our Shepherd leads us in paths of righteousness—not for our name's sake but for His.

Elisabeth Elliot

PRAYER

As we join together in prayer, we draw on God's enabling might in a way that multiplies our own efforts many times over.

Shirley Dobson

The center of power is not to be found in summit meetings or in peace conferences. It is not in Peking or Washington or the United Nations, but rather where a child of God prays in the power of the Spirit for God's will to be done in her life, in her home, and in the world around her.

Ruth Bell Graham

We must leave it to God to answer our prayers in His own wisest way. Sometimes, we are so impatient and think that God does not answer. God always answers! He never fails! Be still. Abide in Him.

Mrs. Charles E. Cowman

When you ask God to do something, don't ask timidly; put your whole heart into it.

Marie T. Freeman

God delights in the prayers of His children—prayers that express our love for Him, prayers that share our deepest burdens with Him.

Billy Graham

Are you weak? Weary? Confused? Troubled? Pressured? How is your relationship with God? Is it held in its place of priority? I believe the greater the pressure, the greater your need for time alone with Him.

Kay Arthur

The Christian on his knees sees more than the philosopher on tiptoe.

D. L. Moody

On our knees we are the most powerful force on earth.

Billy Graham

Prayer guards hearts and minds and causes God to bring peace out of chaos.

Beth Moore

Allow your dreams a place in your prayers and plans. God-given dreams can help you move into the future He is preparing for you.

Barbara Johnson

FORGIVENESS

The fact is, God no longer deals with us in judgment but in mercy. If people got what they deserved, this old planet would have ripped apart at the seams centuries ago. Praise God that because of His great love "we are not consumed, for his compassions never fail" (Lam. 3:22).

Joni Eareckson Tada

When God forgives, He forgets. He buries our sins in the sea and puts a sign on the shore saying, "No Fishing Allowed."

Corrie ten Boom

God expects us to forgive others as He has forgiven us; we are to follow His example by having a forgiving heart.

Vonette Bright

The more you practice the art of forgiving, the quicker you'll master the art of living.

Marie T. Freeman

To hold on to hate and resentments is to throw a monkey wrench into the machinery of life.

E. Stanley Jones

I firmly believe a great many prayers are not answered because we are not willing to forgive someone.

D. L. Moody

It is better to forgive and forget than to resent and remember.

Barbara Johnson

Forgiveness is the precondition of love.

Catherine Marshall

Our relationships with other people are of primary importance to God. Because God is love, He cannot tolerate any unforgiveness or hardness in us toward any individual.

Catherine Marshall

Forgiveness is not an emotion. Forgiveness is an act of the will, and the will can function regardless of the temperature of the heart.

Corrie ten Boom

SERVICE

God wants us to serve Him with a willing spirit, one that would choose no other way.

Beth Moore

No life can surpass that of a man who quietly continues to serve God in the place where providence has placed him.

C. H. Spurgeon

A Christian is a perfectly free lord of all, subject to none. A Christian is a perfectly dutiful servant of all, subject to all.

Martin Luther

If doing a good act in public will excite others to do more good, then "Let your Light shine to all." Miss no opportunity to do good.

John Wesley

You can judge how far you have risen in the scale of life by asking one question: How wisely and how deeply do I care? To be Christianized is to be sensitized. Christians are people who care.

E. Stanley Jones

Doing something positive toward another person is a practical approach to feeling good about yourself.

Barbara Johnson

If you want to discover your spiritual gifts, start obeying God. As you serve Him, you will find that He has given you the gifts that are necessary to follow through in obedience.

Anne Graham Lotz

We can never untangle all the woes in other people's lives. We can't produce miracles overnight. But we can bring a cup of cool water to a thirsty soul, or a scoop of laughter to a lonely heart.

Barbara Johnson

Have thy tools ready;
God will find thee work.

Charles Kingsley

Jesus draws near to those who are suffering—especially when the suffering is for His sake.

Anne Graham Lotz

PRAISE AND THANKSGIVING

Words fail to express my love for this holy Book, my gratitude for its author, for His love and goodness. How shall I thank Him for it?

Lottie Moon

This is my story, this is my song, praising my Savior, all the day long.

Fanny Crosby

Nothing we do is more powerful or more life-changing than praising God.

Stormie Omartian

Our God is the sovereign Creator of the universe! He loves us as His own children and has provided every good thing we have; He is worthy of our praise every moment.

Shirley Dobson

The best moment to praise God is always the present one.

Marie T. Freeman

Preoccupy my thoughts with your praise beginning today.

Joni Eareckson Tada

Two wings are necessary to lift our souls toward God: prayer and praise. Prayer asks. Praise accepts the answer.

Mrs. Charles E. Cowman

The time for universal praise is sure to come some day.
Let us begin to do our part now.

Hannah Whitall Smith

Praise reestablishes the proper chain of command; we recognize that the King is on the throne and that he has saved his people.

Max Lucado

LOVE

Love must be supported and fed and protected, just like a little infant who is growing up at home.

James Dobson

Beware that you are not swallowed up in books! An ounce of love is worth a pound of knowledge.

John Wesley

Brotherly love is still the distinguishing badge of every true Christian.

Matthew Henry

Forgiveness is the final form of love.

Reinhold Niebuhr

How do you spell love? When you reach the point where the happiness, security, and development of another person is as much of a driving force to you as your own happiness, security, and development, then you have a mature love. True love is spelled G-I-V-E. It is not based on what you can get, but rooted in what you can give to the other person.

Josh McDowell

The truth of the Gospel is intended to free us to love God and others with our whole heart.

John Eldredge

Truth becomes hard if it is not softened by love, and love becomes soft if not strengthened by truth.

E. Stanley Jones

Love is not measured by what it gets, but by what it costs.

Oswald Chambers

It is important to know that you have to work to keep love alive; you have to protect it and maintain it, just like you would a delicate flower.

James Dobson

WORSHIP

God actually delights in and pursues our worship (Proverbs 15:8 & John 4:23).

Shirley Dobson

To worship Him in truth means to worship Him honestly, without hypocrisy, standing open and transparent before Him.

Anne Graham Lotz

Inside the human heart is an undeniable, spiritual instinct to commune with its Creator.

Jim Cymbala

Worship is a daunting task. Each worships differently. But each should worship.

Max Lucado

God asks that we worship Him with our concentrated minds as well as with our wills and emotions. A divided and scattered mind is not effective.

Catherine Marshall

Worship is your spirit responding to God's Spirit.

Rick Warren

It is impossible to worship God and remain unchanged.

Henry Blackaby

Praise Him! Praise Him! Tell of His excellent greatness. Praise Him! Praise Him! Ever in joyful song!

Fanny Crosby

Worship is spiritual. Our worship must be more than just outward expression, it must also take place in our spirits.

Franklin Graham

Each time, before you intercede, be quiet first and worship God in His glory. Think of what He can do and how He delights to hear the prayers of His redeemed people. Think of your place and privilege in Christ, and expect great things!

Andrew Murray

ENCOURAGEMENT

Always stay connected to people and seek out things that bring you joy. Dream with abandon. Pray confidently.

Barbara Johnson

The glory of friendship is not the outstretched hand, or the kindly smile, or the joy of companionship. It is the spiritual inspiration that comes to one when he discovers that someone else believes in him and is willing to trust him with his friendship.

Corrie ten Boom

God grant that we may not hinder those who are battling their way slowly into the light.

Oswald Chambers

The truest help we can render an afflicted man is not to take his burden from him, but to call out his best energy, that he may be able to bear the burden himself.

Phillips Brooks

Encouragement starts at home, but it should never end there.

Marie T. Freeman

You can't light another's path without casting light on your own.

John Maxwell

If I am asked how we are to get rid of discouragements, I can only say, as I have had to say of so many other wrong spiritual habits, we must give them up. It is never worth while to argue against discouragement. There is only one argument that can meet it, and that is the argument of God.

Hannah Whitall Smith

A single word, if spoken in a friendly spirit, may be sufficient to turn one from dangerous error.

Fanny Crosby

It is helpful to remember the distinction between appreciation and affirmation. We appreciate what a person does, but we affirm who a person is.

Charles Swindoll

Sometimes one little spark of kindness is all it takes to reignite the light of hope in a heart that's blinded by pain.

Barbara Johnson

ATTITUDE

The things we think are the things that feed our souls. If we think on pure and lovely things, we shall grow pure and lovely like them; and the converse is equally true.

Hannah Whitall Smith

The mind is like a clock that is constantly running down. It has to be wound up daily with good thoughts.

Fulton J. Sheen

The difference between winning and losing is how we choose to react to disappointment.

Barbara Johnson

I have witnessed many attitudes make a positive turnaround through prayer.

John Maxwell

It's your choice: you can either count your blessings or recount your disappointments.

Jim Gallery

The Reference Point for the Christian is the Bible. All values, judgments, and attitudes must be gauged in relationship to this Reference Point.

Ruth Bell Graham

Attitude is the mind's paintbrush; it can color any situation.

Barbara Johnson

Life is 10% what happens to you and 90% how you respond to it.

Charles Swindoll

You've heard the saying, "Life is what you make it." That means we have a choice. We can choose to have a life full of frustration and fear, but we can just as easily choose one of joy and contentment.

Dennis Swanberg

All things being equal, attitude wins. All things not being equal, attitude sometimes still wins.

John Maxwell

JOYFUL CELEBRATION

If you can forgive the person you were, accept the person you are, and believe in the person you will become, you are headed for joy. So celebrate your life.

Barbara Johnson

The Christian lifestyle is not one of legalistic do's and don'ts, but one that is positive, attractive, and joyful.

Vonette Bright

Lord, I thank you for the promise of heaven and the unexpected moments when you touch my heartstrings with that longing for my eternal home.

Joni Eareckson Tada

God knows everything. He can manage everything, and He loves us. Surely this is enough for a fullness of joy that is beyond words.

Hannah Whitall Smith

God gives to us a heavenly gift called joy, radically different in quality from any natural joy.

Elisabeth Elliot

Where the soul is full of peace and joy, outward surroundings and circumstances are of comparatively little account.

Hannah Whitall Smiith

When we get rid of inner conflicts and wrong attitudes toward life, we will almost automatically burst into joy.

E. Stanley Jones

Our God is so wonderfully good, and lovely, and blessed in every way that the mere fact of belonging to Him is enough for an untellable fullness of joy!

Hannah Whitall Smith

He wants us to have a faith that does not complain while waiting, but rejoices because we know our times are in His hands—nail-scarred hands that labor for our highest good.

Kay Arthur

A life of intimacy with God is characterized by joy.

Oswald Chambers

PATIENCE

Waiting is the hardest kind of work, but God knows best, and we may joyfully leave all in His hands.

Lottie Moon

Waiting is an essential part of spiritual discipline. It can be the ultimate test of faith.

Anne Graham Lotz

In the Bible, patience is not a passive acceptance of circumstances. It is a courageous perseverance in the face of suffering and difficulty.

Warren Wiersbe

He makes us wait. He keeps us in the dark on purpose. He makes us walk when we want to run, sit still when we want to walk, for he has things to do in our souls that we are not interested in.

Elisabeth Elliot

When we read of the great Biblical leaders, we see that it was not uncommon for God to ask them to wait, not just a day or two, but for years, until God was ready for them to act.

Gloria Gaither

Wait on the Lord, wait patiently, and thou shalt in Him be blest;
after the storm, a holy calm, and after thy labor rest.

Fanny Crosby

The next time you're disappointed, don't panic. Don't give up. Just be patient and let God remind you he's still in control.

Max Lucado

If God is diligent, surely we ought to be diligent in doing our
duty to Him. Think how patient and diligent God has been to
us!

Oswald Chambers

When I am dealing with an all-powerful, all-knowing God, I, as
a mere mortal, must offer my petitions not only with persistence,
but also with patience. Someday I'll know why.

Ruth Bell Graham

WORLDLINESS

Our fight is not against any physical enemy; it is against organizations and powers that are spiritual. We must struggle against sin all our lives, but we are assured we will win.

Corrie ten Boom

The more we stuff ourselves with material pleasures, the less we seem to appreciate life.

Barbara Johnson

All those who look to draw their satisfaction from the wells of the world—pleasure, popularity, position, possessions, politics, power, prestige, finances, family, friends, fame, fortune, career, children, church, clubs, sports, sex, success, recognition, reputation, religion, education, entertainment, exercise, honors, health, hobbies—will soon be thirsty again!

Anne Graham Lotz

The Lord Jesus Christ is still praying for us. He wants us to be in the world but not of it.

Charles Stanley

The only ultimate disaster that can befall us, I have come to realize, is to feel ourselves to be home on earth.

Max Lucado

The true Christian, though he is in revolt against the world's efforts to brainwash him, is no mere rebel for rebellion's sake. He dissents from the world because he knows that it cannot make good on its promises.

A. W. Tozer

It is impossible to please God doing things motivated by and produced by the flesh.

Bill Bright

The world's sewage system threatens to contaminate the stream of Christian thought. Is the world shaping your mind, or is Christ?

Billy Graham

Our joy ends where love of the world begins.

C. H. Spurgeon

There is no hell on earth like horizontal living without God.

Charles Swindoll

WORRY

Worry is the senseless process of cluttering up tomorrow's opportunities with leftover problems from today.

Barbara Johnson

Never yield to gloomy anticipation. Place your hope and confidence in God. He has no record of failure.

Mrs. Charles E. Cowman

Pray, and let God worry.

Martin Luther

Today is mine. Tomorrow is none of my business. If I peer anxiously into the fog of the future, I will strain my spiritual eyes so that I will not see clearly what is required of me now.

Elisabeth Elliott

Worry and anxiety are sand in the machinery of life; faith is the oil.

E. Stanley Jones

Anxiety may be natural and normal for the world, but it is not to be part of a believer's lifestyle.

Kay Arthur

Worries carry responsibilities that belong to God, not to you. Worry does not enable us to escape evil; it makes us unfit to cope with it when it comes.

Corrie ten Boom

I've read the last page of the Bible. It's all going to turn out all right.

Billy Graham

We are not called to be burden-bearers,
but cross-bearers and light-bearers.
We must cast our burdens on the Lord.

Corrie ten Boom

This life of faith, then, consists in just this—being a child in the Father's house. Let the ways of childish confidence and freedom from care, which so please you and win your heart when you observe your own little ones, teach you what you should be in your attitude toward God.

Hannah Whitall Smith

SELF-DISCIPLINE

"They that sow bountifully shall reap also bountifully," is as true in spiritual things as in material.

Lottie Moon

Work is doing it. Discipline is doing it every day. Diligence is doing it well every day.

Dave Ramsey

Personal humility is a spiritual discipline and the hallmark of the service of Jesus.

Franklin Graham

As we make an offering of our work, we find the truth of a principle Jesus taught: Fulfillment is not a goal to achieve, but always the by-product of a sacrifice.

Elisabeth Elliot

Working in the vineyard, Working all the day, Never be discouraged, Only watch and pray.

Fanny Crosby

Father was the old-fashioned sort who believed that the authority in the home belonged to parents and not to the children. He was in favor of the posterior application of superior force if necessary.

Vance Havner

You can't climb the ladder of life with your hands in your pockets.

Barbara Johnson

The alternative to discipline is disaster.

Vance Havner

Obedience to God is our job. The results of that obedience are God's.

Elisabeth Elliot

The secret of a happy life is to delight in duty. When duty becomes delight, then burdens become blessings.

Warren Wiersbe

LIVING PURPOSEFULLY

His life is our light—our purpose and meaning and reason for living.

Anne Graham Lotz

Yesterday is just experience but tomorrow is glistening with purpose—and today is the channel leading from one to the other.

Barbara Johnson

Only God's chosen task for you will ultimately satisfy. Do not wait until it is too late to realize the privilege of serving Him in His chosen position for you.

Beth Moore

In the very place where God has put us, whatever its limitations, whatever kind of work it may be, we may indeed serve the Lord Christ.

Elisabeth Elliot

How much of our lives are, well, so daily. How often our hours are filled with the mundane, seemingly unimportant things that have to be done, whether at home or work. These very "daily" tasks could become a celebration of praise. "It is through consecration," someone has said, "that drudgery is made divine."

Gigi Graham Tchividjian

God is more concerned with the direction of your life than with its speed.

Marie T. Freeman

God specializes in things fresh and firsthand. His plans for you this year may outshine those of the past. He's prepared to fill your days with reasons to give Him praise.

Joni Eareckson Tada

Oh Lord, let me not live to be useless.

John Wesley

Without God, life has no purpose, and without purpose, life has no meaning.

Rick Warren

Whatever purpose motivates your life, it must be something big enough and grand enough to make the investment worthwhile.

Warren Wiersbe

Read the Bible in a Year

January

1 Genesis 1-2 Matthew 1	2 Genesis 3-5 Matthew 2	3 Genesis 6-8 Matthew 3	4 Genesis 9-11 Matthew 4
5 Genesis 12-14 Matthew 5:1-20	6 Genesis 15-17 Matthew 5:21-48	7 Genesis 18-19 Matthew 6:1-18	8 Genesis 20-21 Matthew 6:19-34
9 Genesis 22-25 Matthew 7	10 Genesis 26-27 Matthew 8:1-20	11 Genesis 28-29 Matthew 8:21-34	12 Genesis 30-31 Matthew 9:1-17
13 Genesis 32-33 Matthew 9:18-38	14 Genesis 34-35 Matthew 10:1-24	15 Genesis 36-38 Matthew 10:25-42	16 Genesis 39-40 Matthew 11
17 Genesis 41-42 Matthew 12:1-24	18 Genesis 43-44 Matthew 12:25-50	19 Genesis 45-46 Matthew 13:1-36	20 Genesis 47-48 Matthew 13:37-58
21 Genesis 49-50 Matthew 14	22 Exodus 1-3 Matthew 15:1-20	23 Exodus 4-6 Matthew 15:21-39	24 Exodus 7-9 Matthew 16
25 Exodus 10-12 Matthew 17	26 Exodus 13-14 Matthew 18:1-20	27 Exodus 15-16 Matthew 18:21-35	28 Exodus 17-18 Matthew 19
29 Exodus 19-20 Matthew 20:1-16	30 Exodus 21-22 Matthew 20:17-34	31 Exodus 23-24 Matthew 21:1-22	

Thoughts for the Month

FEBRUARY

1 Exodus 25-27 Matthew 21:23-46	2 Exodus 28-30 Matthew 22:1-22	3 Exodus 31-33 Matthew 22:23-46	4 Exodus 34-35 Matthew 23
5 Exodus 36-37 Matthew 24:1-28	6 Exodus 38-39 Matthew 24:29-51	7 Exodus 40 Matthew 25	8 Leviticus 1-2 Matthew 26:1-29
9 Leviticus 3-4 Matthew 26:30-56	10 Leviticus 5-6 Matthew 26:57-75	11 Leviticus 7-8 Matthew 27:1-26	12 Leviticus 9-10 Matthew 27:27-53
13 Leviticus 11-12 Matthew 27:54-66	14 Leviticus 13-14 Matthew 28	15 Leviticus 15-16 Mark 1:1-28	16 Leviticus 17-18 Mark 1:29-45
17 Leviticus 19-20 Mark 2	18 Leviticus 21-22 Mark 3:1-19	19 Leviticus 23-24 Mark 3:20-35	20 Leviticus 25 Mark 4:1-20
21 Leviticus 26-27 Mark 4:21-41	22 Numbers 1-2 Mark 5:1-19	23 Numbers 3-4 Mark 5:20-43	24 Numbers 5-6 Mark 6:1-12
25 Numbers 7-9 Mark 6:13-32	26 Numbers 10-12 Mark 6:33-56	27 Numbers 13-15 Mark 7:1-13	28 Numbers 16-18 Mark 7:14-37

THOUGHTS FOR THE MONTH

MARCH

1 Numbers 19-21 Mark 8:1-13	2 Numbers 22-24 Mark 8:14-38	3 Numbers 25-27 Mark 9:1-29	4 Numbers 28-30 Mark 9:30-50
5 Numbers 31-33 Mark 10:1-31	6 Numbers 34-36 Mark 10:32-52	7 Deuteronomy 1-3 Mark 11:1-19	8 Deuteronomy 4-6 Mark 11:20-33
9 Deuteronomy 7-9 Mark 12:1-28	10 Deuteronomy 10-12 Mark 12:29-44	11 Deuteronomy 13-15 Mark 13	12 Deuteronomy 16-18 Mark 14:1-9
13 Deuteronomy 19-21 Mark 14:10-36	14 Deuteronomy 22-24 Mark 14:37-72	15 Deuteronomy 25-27 Mark 15:1-26	16 Deuteronomy 28-30 Mark 15:27-47
17 Deuteronomy 31-32 Mark 16	18 Deuteronomy 33-34 Luke 1:1-38	19 Joshua 1-3 Luke 1:39-80	20 Joshua 4-6 Luke 2:1-24
21 Joshua 7-9 Luke 2:25-52	22 Joshua 10-12 Luke 3:1-18	23 Joshua 13-15 Luke 3:19-38	24 Joshua 16-18 Luke 4:1-13
25 Joshua 19-21 Luke 4:14-30	26 Joshua 22-24 Luke 4:31-44	27 Judges 1-2 Luke 5:1-16	28 Judges 3-5 Luke 5:17-39
29 Judges 6-8 Luke 6:1-18	30 Judges 9-11 Luke 6:19-49	31 Judges 12-13 Luke 7:1-28	

THOUGHTS FOR THE MONTH

1 Judges 14-15 Luke 7:29-50	2 Judges 16-17 Luke 8:1-21	3 Judges 18-19 Luke 8:22-40	4 Judges 20-21 Luke 8:41-56
5 Ruth 1-2 Luke 9:1-17	6 Ruth 3-4 Luke 9:18-36	7 1 Samuel 1-3 Luke 9:37-62	8 1 Samuel 4-6 Luke 10:1-24
9 1 Samuel 7-9 Luke 10:25-42	10 1 Samuel 10-12 Luke 11:1-36	11 1 Samuel 13-15 Luke 11:37-54	12 1 Samuel 16-18 Luke 12:1-40
13 1 Samuel 19-21 Luke 12:41-59	14 1 Samuel 22-24 Luke 13:1-21	15 1 Samuel 25-27 Luke 13:22-35	16 1 Samuel 28-29 Luke 14:1-14
17 1 Samuel 30-31 Luke 14:15-35	18 2 Samuel 1-3 Luke 15	19 2 Samuel 4-6 Luke 16:1-13	20 2 Samuel 7-9 Luke 16:14-31
21 2 Samuel 10-12 Luke 17:1-19	22 2 Samuel 13-15 Luke 17:20-37	23 2 Samuel 16-18 Luke 18:1-17	24 2 Samuel 19-21 Luke 18:18-43
25 2 Samuel 22-24 Luke 19:1-27	26 1 Kings 1-2 Luke 19:28-48	27 1 Kings 3-4 Luke 20:1-18	28 1 Kings 5-6 Luke 20:19-47
29 1 Kings 7-8 Luke 21	30 1 Kings 9-10 Luke 22:1-22		

THOUGHTS FOR THE MONTH

1	2	3	4
1 Kings 11-12	1 Kings 13-14	1 Kings 15-16	1 Kings 17-18
Luke 22:23-53	Luke 22:54-71	Luke 23:1-25	Luke 23:26-56
5	6	7	8
1 Kings 19-20	1 Kings 21-22	2 Kings 1-2	2 Kings 3-5
Luke 24:1-20	Luke 24:21-36	Luke 24:37-53	John 1:1-28
9	10	11	12
2 Kings 6-8	2 Kings 9-11	2 Kings 12-13	2 Kings 14-16
John 1:29-51	John 2	John 3:1-21	John 3:22-36
13	14	15	16
2 Kings 17-19	2 Kings 20-21	2 Kings 22-23	2 Kings 24-25
John 4:1-30	John 4:31-54	John 5:1-18	John 5:19-47
17	18	19	20
1 Chronicles 1-3	1 Chronicles 4-6	1 Chronicles 7-9	1 Chronicles 10-12
John 6:1-21	John 6:22-40	John 6:41-58	John 6:59-71
21	22	23	24
1 Chronicles 13-15	1 Chronicles 16-18	1 Chronicles 19-21	1 Chronicles 22-24
John 7:1-32	John 7:33-53	John 8:1-30	John 8:31-59
25	26	27	28
1 Chronicles 25-26	1 Chronicles 27-29	2 Chronicles 1-2	2 Chronicles 3-5
John 9	John 10:1-18	John 10:19-42	John 11:1-29
29	30	31	
2 Chronicles 6-8	2 Chronicles 9-11	2 Chronicles 12-14	
John 11:30-57	John 12:1-16	John 12:17-36	

THOUGHTS FOR THE MONTH

JUNE

1 2 Chronicles 15-17 John 12:37-50	2 2 Chronicles 18-19 John 13:1-20	3 2 Chronicles 20-21 John 13:21-38	4 2 Chronicles 22-23 John 14
5 2 Chronicles 24-25 John 15	6 2 Chronicles 26-27 John 16	7 2 Chronicles 28-29 John 17	8 2 Chronicles 30-31 John 18:1-19
9 2 Chronicles 32-34 John 18:20-40	10 2 Chronicles 35-36 John 19:1-28	11 Ezra 1-3 John 19:29-42	12 Ezra 4-6 John 20
13 Ezra 7-8 John 21	14 Ezra 9-10 Acts 1	15 Nehemiah 1-2 Acts 2	16 Nehemiah 3-5 Acts 3
17 Nehemiah 6-8 Acts 4	18 Nehemiah 9-10 Acts 5	19 Nehemiah 11-13 Acts 6	20 Esther 1-3 Acts 7:1-39
21 Esther 4-5 Acts 7:40-60	22 Esther 6-7 Acts 8:1-13	23 Esther 8-10 Acts 8:14-40	24 Job 1-3 Acts 9:1-22
25 Job 4-5 Acts 9:23-43	26 Job 6-7 Acts 10:1-23	27 Job 8-9 Acts 10:24-48	28 Job 10-11 Acts 11:1-18
29 Job 12-14 Acts 11:19-30	30 Job 15-17 Acts 12		

THOUGHTS FOR THE MONTH

JULY

1 Job 18-20 Acts 13:1-12	2 Job 21-23 Acts 13:13-31	3 Job 24-26 Acts 13:32-52	4 Job 27-29 Acts 14
5 Job 30-32 Acts 15:1-21	6 Job 33-34 Acts 15:22-41	7 Job 35-36 Acts 16:1-22	8 Job 37-38 Acts 16:23-40
9 Job 39-40 Acts 17:1-15	10 Job 41-42 Acts 17:16-34	11 Psalms 1-3 Acts 18	12 Psalms 4-6 Acts 19
13 Psalms 7-8 Acts 20	14 Psalms 9-11 Acts 21:1-17	15 Psalms 12-14 Acts 21:18-40	16 Psalms 15-17 Acts 22:1-11
17 Psalms 18 Acts 22:12-30	18 Psalms 19-20 Acts 23:1-11	19 Psalms 21-22 Acts 23:12-35	20 Psalms 23-25 Acts 24
21 Psalms 26-27 Acts 25	22 Psalms 28-29 Acts 26	23 Psalms 30-33 Acts 27:1-18	24 Psalms 34-35 Acts 27:19-44
25 Psalms 36-38 Acts 28:1-10	26 Psalms 39-41 Acts 28:11-31	27 Psalms 42-44 Romans 1	28 Psalms 45-46 Romans 2
29 Psalms 47-48 Romans 3	30 Psalms 49-50 Romans 4	31 Psalms 51-53 Romans 5	

THOUGHTS FOR THE MONTH

1 Psalms 54-57 Romans 6	2 Psalms 58-60 Romans 7	3 Psalms 61-64 Romans 8:1-21	4 Psalms 65-66 Romans 8:22-39
5 Psalms 67-68 Romans 9:1-16	6 Psalms 69 Romans 9:17-33	7 Psalms 70-72 Romans 10	8 Psalms 73-74 Romans 11:1-21
9 Psalms 75-77 Romans 11:22-36	10 Psalms 78 Romans 12	11 Psalms 79-81 Romans 13	12 Psalms 82-85 Romans 14
13 Psalms 86-88 Romans 15:1-13	14 Psalms 89 Romans 15:14-21	15 Psalms 90-93 Romans 15:22-33	16 Psalms 94-97 Romans 16
17 Psalms 98-100 1 Corinthians 1	18 Psalms 101-103 1 Corinthians 2	19 Psalms 104-105 1 Corinthians 3	20 Psalms 106 1 Corinthians 4
21 Psalms 107-109 1 Corinthians 5	22 Psalms 110-113 1 Corinthians 6	23 Psalms 114-118 1 Corinthians 7	24 Psalms 119:1-72 1 Corinthians 8
25 Psalms 119:73-176 1 Corinthians 9	26 Psalms 120-123 1 Corinthians 10:1-13	27 Psalms 124-127 1 Corinthians 10:14-33	28 Psalms 128-132 1 Corinthians 11:1-18
29 Psalms 133-135 1 Corinthians 11:19-34	30 Psalms 136-138 1 Corinthians 12:1-18	31 Psalms 139 1 Corinthians 12:19-31	

Thoughts for the Month

September

1	2	3	4
Psalms 140-142 1 Corinthians 13	Psalms 143-145 1 Corinthians 14:1-19	Psalms 146-147 1 Corinthians 14:20-40	Psalms 148-150 1 Corinthians 15:1-11
5 Proverbs 1 1 Corinthians 15:12-25	6 Proverbs 2-3 1 Corinthians 15:26-58	7 Proverbs 4-5 1 Corinthians 16	8 Proverbs 6-7 2 Corinthians 1
9 Proverbs 8-9 2 Corinthians 2	10 Proverbs 10-11 2 Corinthians 3	11 Proverbs 12-13 2 Corinthians 4	12 Proverbs 14-15 2 Corinthians 5
13 Proverbs 16-17 2 Corinthians 6	14 Proverbs 18-19 2 Corinthians 7-8	15 Proverbs 20-21 2 Corinthians 9	16 Proverbs 22-23 2 Corinthians 10
17 Proverbs 24-25 2 Corinthians 11:1-11	18 Proverbs 26-27 2 Corinthians 11:12-33	19 Proverbs 28-29 2 Corinthians 12	20 Proverbs 30-31 2 Corinthians 13
21 Ecclesiastes 1-3 Galatians 1	22 Ecclesiastes 4-6 Galatians 2	23 Ecclesiastes 7-8 Galatians 3	24 Ecclesiastes 9-12 Galatians 4
25 Song of Solomon 1-4 Galatians 5	26 Song of Solomon 5-8 Galatians 6	27 Isaiah 1-2 Ephesians 1	28 Isaiah 3-4 Ephesians 2
29 Isaiah 5-6 Ephesians 3	30 Isaiah 7-8 Ephesians 4		

Thoughts for the Month

OCTOBER

1 Isaiah 9-10 Ephesians 5	2 Isaiah 11-12 Ephesians 6	3 Isaiah 13-14 Philippians 1	4 Isaiah 15-16 Philippians 2
5 Isaiah 17-19 Philippians 3	6 Isaiah 20-22 Philippians 4	7 Isaiah 23-25 Colossians 1	8 Isaiah 26-27 Colossians 2
9 Isaiah 28-29 Colossians 3	10 Isaiah 30-31 Colossians 4	11 Isaiah 32-33 1 Thessalonians 1	12 Isaiah 34-35 1 Thessalonians 2
13 Isaiah 36-37 1 Thessalonians 3	14 Isaiah 38-39 1 Thessalonians 4	15 Isaiah 40-42 1 Thessalonians 5	16 Isaiah 43-45 2 Thessalonians 1
17 Isaiah 46-48 2 Thessalonians 2	18 Isaiah 49-51 2 Thessalonians 3	19 Isaiah 52-54 1 Timothy 1	20 Isaiah 55-57 1 Timothy 2
21 Isaiah 58-60 1 Timothy 3	22 Isaiah 61-63 1 Timothy 4	23 Isaiah 64-66 1 Timothy 5	24 Jeremiah 1-3 1 Timothy 6
25 Jeremiah 4-6 2 Timothy 1	26 Jeremiah 7-9 2 Timothy 2	27 Jeremiah 10-12 2 Timothy 3	28 Jeremiah 13-15 2 Timothy 4
29 Jeremiah 16-18 Titus 1	30 Jeremiah 19-20 Titus 2	31 Jeremiah 21-22 Titus 3	

THOUGHTS FOR THE MONTH

November

1 Jeremiah 23-24 Philemon	2 Jeremiah 25-27 Hebrews 1	3 Jeremiah 28-30 Hebrews 2	4 Jeremiah 31-32 Hebrews 3
5 Jeremiah 33-35 Hebrews 4	6 Jeremiah 36-38 Hebrews 5	7 Jeremiah 39-41 Hebrews 6	8 Jeremiah 42-44 Hebrews 7
9 Jeremiah 45-47 Hebrews 8	10 Jeremiah 48-49 Hebrews 9	11 Jeremiah 50 Hebrews 10:1-22	12 Jeremiah 51 Hebrews 10:23-39
13 Jeremiah 52 Hebrews 11:1-16	14 Lamentations 1-2 Hebrews 11:17-40	15 Lamentations 3-5 Hebrews 12:1-13	16 Ezekiel 1-2 Hebrews 12:14-29
17 Ezekiel 3-5 Hebrews 13	18 Ezekiel 6-7 James 1	19 Ezekiel 8-10 James 2	20 Ezekiel 11-13 James 3
21 Ezekiel 14-16 James 4	22 Ezekiel 17-18 James 5	23 Ezekiel 19-20 1 Peter 1	24 Ezekiel 21-22 1 Peter 2
25 Ezekiel 23-24 1 Peter 3	26 Ezekiel 25-27 1 Peter 4	27 Ezekiel 28-30 1 Peter 5	28 Ezekiel 31-33 2 Peter 1
29 Ezekiel 34-36 2 Peter 2	30 Ezekiel 37-39 2 Peter 3		

Thoughts for the Month

December

1 Ezekiel 40-41 1 John 1	2 Ezekiel 42-44 1 John 2	3 Ezekiel 45-46 1 John 3	4 Ezekiel 47-48 1 John 4
5 Daniel 1-2 1 John 5	6 Daniel 3-4 2 John	7 Daniel 5-6 3 John	8 Daniel 7-8 Jude
9 Daniel 9-10 Revelation 1	10 Daniel 11-12 Revelation 2	11 Hosea 1-3 Revelation 3	12 Hosea 4-7 Revelation 4
13 Hosea 8-11 Revelation 5	14 Hosea 12-14 Revelation 6	15 Joel 1-3 Revelation 7	16 Amos 1-4 Revelation 8
17 Amos 5-9 Revelation 9	18 Obadiah Revelation 10	19 Jonah 1-4 Revelation 11	20 Micah 1-3 Revelation 12
21 Micah 4-5 Revelation 13	22 Micah 6-7 Revelation 14	23 Nahum 1-3 Revelation 15	24 Habakkuk 1-3 Revelation 16
25 Zephaniah 1-3 Revelation 17	26 Haggai 1-2 Revelation 18	27 Zechariah 1-4 Revelation 19	28 Zechariah 5-8 Revelation 20
29 Zechariah 9-11 Revelation 21	30 Zechariah 12-14 Revelation 22:1-8	31 Malachi 1-4 Revelation 22:9-21	

Thoughts for the Month

READ THE BIBLE IN 52 WEEKS

Week 1	Week 2	Week 3
Genesis 1-18	Genesis 19-35	Genesis 36-50
Matthew 1-7	Matthew 8-10	Matthew 11-14
Week 4	Week 5	Week 6
Exodus 1-18	Exodus 19-35	Exodus 36-Leviticus 8
Matthew 15-19	Matthew 20-23	Matthew 24-27
Week 7	Week 8	Week 9
Leviticus 9-22	Leviticus 23-Numbers 9	Numbers 10-30
Matthew 28-Mark 4	Mark 5-6	Mark 7-9
Week 10	Week 11	Week 12
Numbers 31-Deuteronomy 15	Deuteronomy 16-34	Joshua 1-21
Mark 10-13	Mark 14-16	Luke 1-5
Week 13	Week 14	Week 15
Joshua 22-Judges 15	Judges 16-1 Samuel 6	1 Samuel 7-1 Samuel 27
Luke 6-8	Luke 9-11	Luke 12-14
Week 16	Week 17	Week 18
1 Samuel 28-2 Samuel 15	2 Samuel 16-1 Kings 8	1 Kings 9-2 Kings 2
Luke 15-17	Luke 18-21	Luke 22-24
Week 19	Week 20	Week 21
2 Kings 3-2 Kings 20	2 Kings 21-1 Chronicles 12	1 Chronicles 13-29
John 1-4	John 5-7	John 8-10
Week 22	Week 23	Week 24
2 Chronicles 1-21	2 Chronicles 22-36	Ezra 1-Nehemiah 13
John 11-13	John 14-19	John 20-Acts 5
Week 25	Week 26	Week 27
Esther 1-Job 5	Job 6-23	Job 24-Job 40
Acts 6-9	Acts 10-13	Acts 14-17

Week 28 Job 41-Psalm 17 Acts 18-21	Week 29 Psalm 18-31 Acts 22-26	Week 30 Psalm 32-50 Acts 27-Romans 4
Week 31 Psalm 51-68 Romans 5-9	Week 32 Psalm 69-85 Romans 10-14	Week 33 Psalm 86-105 Romans 15-1 Corinthians 3
Week 34 Psalm 106-124 1 Corinthians 4-10	Week 35 Psalm 125-145 1 Corinthians 11-14	Week 36 Psalm 146-Proverbs 9 1 Cor 15-2 Cor 2
Week 37 Proverbs 10-23 2 Corinthians 3-10	Week 38 Proverbs 24-Ecclesiastes 8 2 Corinthians 11-Galatians 3	Week 39 Ecclesiastes 9-Isaiah 7 Galatians 4-Ephesians 4
Week 40 Isaiah 8-26 Ephesians 5-Colossians 1	Week 41 Isaiah 27-45 Colossians 2-1 Thessalonians 5	Week 42 Isaiah 46-66 2 Thessalonians 1-1 Timothy 6
Week 43 Jeremiah 1-15 2 Timothy 1-Titus 3	Week 44 Jeremiah 16-36 Philemon-Hebrews 6	Week 45 Jeremiah 37-52 Hebrews 7-11
Week 46 Lamentations 1- Ezekiel 16 Hebrews 12-James 3	Week 47 Ezekiel 17-33 James 4-1 Peter 5	Week 48 Ezekiel 34-48 2 Peter 1-1 John 5
Week 49 Daniel 1-Hosea 3 2 John-Jude	Week 50 Hosea 4-Amos 9 Revelation 1-10	Week 51 Obadiah-Zephaniah 3 Revelation 11-18
Week 52 Haggai 1-Malachi 4 Revelation 19-22		